Georgia
Milestones
Grade 6
Mathematics
SUCCESS STRATEGIES

**Georgia Milestones Test
Review for the
Georgia Milestones
Assessment System**

Dear Future Exam Success Story:

Congratulations on your purchase of our study guide. Our goal in writing our study guide was to cover the content on the test, as well as provide insight into typical test taking mistakes and how to overcome them.

Standardized tests are a key component of being successful, which only increases the importance of doing well in the high-pressure high-stakes environment of test day. How well you do on this test will have a significant impact on your future, and we have the research and practical advice to help you execute on test day.

The product you're reading now is designed to exploit weaknesses in the test itself, and help you avoid the most common errors test takers frequently make.

How to use this study guide

We don't want to waste your time. Our study guide is fast-paced and fluff-free. We suggest going through it a number of times, as repetition is an important part of learning new information and concepts.

First, read through the study guide completely to get a feel for the content and organization. Read the general success strategies first, and then proceed to the content sections. Each tip has been carefully selected for its effectiveness.

Second, read through the study guide again, and take notes in the margins and highlight those sections where you may have a particular weakness.

Finally, bring the manual with you on test day and study it before the exam begins.

Your success is our success

We would be delighted to hear about your success. Send us an email and tell us your story. Thanks for your business and we wish you continued success.

Sincerely,

Mometrix Test Preparation Team

Need more help? Check out our flashcards at:
http://mometrixflashcards.com/GeorgiaMilestones

TABLE OF CONTENTS

Top 15 Test Taking Tips

1. Know the test directions, duration, topics, question types, how many questions
2. Setup a flexible study schedule at least 3-4 weeks before test day
3. Study during the time of day you are most alert, relaxed, and stress free
4. Maximize your learning style; visual learner use visual study aids, auditory learner use auditory study aids
5. Focus on your weakest knowledge base
6. Find a study partner to review with and help clarify questions
7. Practice, practice, practice
8. Get a good night's sleep; don't try to cram the night before the test
9. Eat a well balanced meal
10. Wear comfortable, loose fitting, layered clothing; prepare for it to be either cold or hot during the test
11. Eliminate the obviously wrong answer choices, then guess the first remaining choice
12. Pace yourself; don't rush, but keep working and move on if you get stuck
13. Maintain a positive attitude even if the test is going poorly
14. Keep your first answer unless you are positive it is wrong
15. Check your work, don't make a careless mistake

Geometry

Coordinate grid

<u>Example problem 1</u>

Your neighborhood can be represented by a coordinate grid, with each unit representing 1 block. Your house is located at (1,5), the park is located at (5,5), the drug store is located at (5,0), and the gas station is located at (1,0). Each morning you go for a run from your house along a route to the park, then the drug store, the gas station, and then back home. Plot this route on a coordinate grid and determine how many blocks you run.

You run 18 blocks on this route:

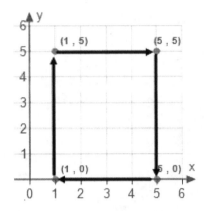

With each dot representing a location in your neighborhood, the route forms a rectangle. The first part of the route is 4 blocks to get from your house to the park, then 5 blocks to get from the park to the drug store, 4 more blocks to get from the drug store to the gas station, and finally 5 blocks to get from the gas station back to your house. Adding all these together gives you $4 + 5 + 4 + 5 = 18$ blocks. These distances can be found by either counting the number of squares on the grid between each location, or by finding the distance between the x or y coordinates (depending whether you're moving horizontally or vertically on the graph, respectively) of two points. For example, the distance between your house at (1,5) and the park at (5,5) is $5 - 1 = 4$ blocks, because you need to go 4 blocks over to get from the x-coordinate of 1 to the x-coordinate of 5, while not moving y-coordinates at all.

Surface area and volume

Example problem 1

Find the Surface Area and Volume of a cube with side of length 3cm given the following formulas:
$$SA = 6s^2 \quad and \quad V = s^3$$

The Surface Area of the cube is 54 square cm and the Volume of the cube is 27 cubic cm. In a cube, the length, width, and height are all the same measurement, which is why the formulas only have one variable, s, which refers to the length of each side. The answers are found by substituting 3 for s in each formula. Surface Area: $SA = 6 \times 3^2 = 6 \times 9 = 54cm^2$. Volume: $V = 3^3 = 27cm^3$.

Example problem 2

Find the Surface Area and Volume of a cylinder with a height of 4cm and radius of 6cm, given the formulas below.
$$SA = 2\pi r^2 + 2\pi rh \quad and \quad V = \pi r^2 h$$

The Surface Area of the cylinder is 120π square cm and the Volume of the cylinder is 144π cubic cm. Substitute 4 for h in each formula, since h represents the height, and 6 for r in each formula, since r represents the radius. Surface Area:
$SA = 2\pi \times 6^2 + 2\pi \times 6 \times 4 = 2\pi \times 36 + 2\pi \times 24 = 72\pi + 48\pi = 120\pi \ cm^2$.
Volume: $V = \pi \times 6^2 \times 4 = \pi \times 36 \times 4 = 144\pi \ cm^3$.

Area

Example problem 1
Find the area of the following isosceles trapezoid:

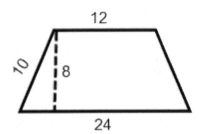

The area of the trapezoid is 144 square units and can be found by breaking the shape into two triangles and one rectangle, like so:
- Since the top base of the trapezoid has a length of 12 and is also the top of the rectangle, then the bottom of the rectangle also has a length of 12. Because the whole base had a length of 24, this leaves 12 for the two bases of the triangles. Dividing this remaining portion in half (because we are told the trapezoid is isosceles) gives each triangle a base of 6. The area of the rectangle is $12 \times 8 = 96$, and the area of each triangle is $\frac{6 \times 8}{2} = \frac{48}{2} = 24$. The total area is then $96 + 24 + 24 = 144$ square units.

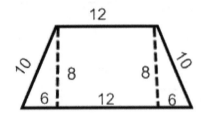

Example problem 2

Jeremy is staining the cement floor in his basement. He wants to stain the shape of a hexagon in the middle of the floor. He outlines a regular hexagon that has a side of length 6 feet on all sides and a height of 10.4 feet. Find the area Jeremy needs enough stain to cover.

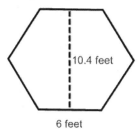

6 feet

Jeremy will need enough stain to cover 93.6 square feet. This area of the hexagon is found by breaking the hexagon into 6 triangles. Because it is a regular hexagon, each side length is 6 and the height of one triangle is half the height of the whole hexagon, or $\frac{10.4}{2} = 5.2$. Therefore all the triangles are congruent as seen in the diagram below:

Using the formula for area of a triangle, $A = \frac{b \times h}{2}$, each triangle has an area of $\frac{6 \times 5.2}{2} = \frac{31.2}{2} = 15.6$ square feet. Since each of the 6 triangles has the same area, the total area of the hexagon is then $15.6 \times 6 = 93.6$ square feet.

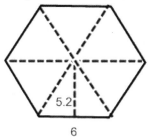

6

Example problem 3

Find the area of the right triangle that has its longest side connecting points A (3, 8) and B (9, 4), and has one horizontal leg and one vertical leg.

The area of this triangle is 12 square units.

To solve for the area, it may be helpful to draw a diagram. Since we are told one leg is horizontal and the other vertical, the legs of the right triangle meet at the ordered pair (3, 4) (or at (9, 8) which would give the same area). The height of the triangle is the distance from (3, 4) to point A at (3, 8) which is 4 units. The base of the triangle is the distance from (3, 4) to point B at (9, 4) which is 6 units. The area of a triangle is found by the formula $A = \frac{b \times h}{2}$ and for this triangle the area is $A = \frac{6 \times 4}{2} = \frac{24}{2} = 12$ units^2.

Volume

Example Problem 1

Ryland Raisin Company is creating new mini-boxes of raisins to sell at school lunches. They have decided to package them in a box that is a cube with dimensions of $\frac{4}{3}in \times \frac{4}{3}in \times \frac{4}{3}in$. Find how many mini-boxes with side lengths of $\frac{1}{3}in$ can fit into a raisin box package and what volume the larger box can hold.

There are 64 cubes with side lengths of $\frac{1}{3}$ in that can fit into this new raisin box. The volume of the box is $\frac{64}{27}in^3 = 2\frac{10}{27}in^3$.

The number of $\frac{1}{3}$ in sided cubes that fit into the box can be found by creating a diagram of the box with its dimensions broken down into $\frac{1}{3}in$ portions as seen below:

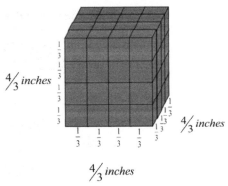

The top row of the box shows there are 16 cubes with sides of $\frac{1}{3}in$. There are 4 of these rows, which makes a total of $16 \times 4 = 64$ cubes. Since the volume of each little cube is $\frac{1}{3} \times \frac{1}{3} \times \frac{1}{3} = \frac{1}{27}in^3$, then the total volume is $64 \times \frac{1}{27} = \frac{64}{27} = 2\frac{10}{27}in^3$. This total volume can also be found by multiplying the dimensions of the raisin box package directly: $\frac{4}{3} \times \frac{4}{3} \times \frac{4}{3} = \frac{64}{27} = 2\frac{10}{27}in^3$.

Example problem 2

At the grocery store you see two different kinds of cereal on sale for the same price. Box A has dimensions $\frac{3}{4}ft \times \frac{1}{2}ft \times \frac{2}{3}ft$ and Box B has dimensions $\frac{9}{10}ft \times \frac{1}{3}ft \times \frac{4}{5}ft$. Decide which box will give you the most cereal for your money.

Box A will give you more cereal for your money because the box can hold more volume than Box B. Find the volume of each box using the formula $V = l \times w \times h$. The volume of Box A is $\frac{3}{4} \times \frac{1}{2} \times \frac{2}{3} = \frac{6}{24} = \frac{1}{4}ft^3$, and the volume of Box B is $\frac{9}{10} \times \frac{1}{3} \times \frac{4}{5} = \frac{36}{150} = \frac{6}{25}ft^3$. Because $\frac{1}{4} = .25$ and $\frac{6}{25} = .24$, the volume of Box A is slightly larger than the volume of Box B and therefore a better deal because it will hold more cereal.

<u>Example problem 3</u>

An isosceles right triangle has a hypotenuse of 10 units. What is the area of the triangle?

An isosceles right triangle has congruent leg lengths. Apply the Pythagorean Theorem, which states that the sum of the squares of the lengths of the legs is equal to the square of the length of the hypotenuse:

$a^2 + b^2 = c^2$ Pythagorean Theorem
$b^2 + b^2 = 10^2$ The legs are congruent, so use b for each leg length.
$2b^2 = 100$
$b^2 = 50$
$b = \sqrt{50}$

The area of the triangle is one half the base times the height, or in this case $A = \frac{1}{2}b^2$, where $b^2 = 50$. The area of the triangle is therefore 25 square units.

Net figure

<u>Example problem 1</u>

Sheila is going to make her own canvas tent for camping. She wants to make a tent that is the shape of a triangular prism. Given the dimensions below, create a net figure of the tent and determine how much canvas Sheila will need to make it.

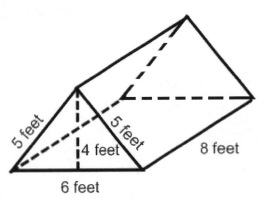

Sheila will need 152 square feet of canvas. This is found by determining the surface area of the triangular prism. In the net figure below, it is clear to see that the sum of the areas of two triangles and three rectangles will give the full surface area.

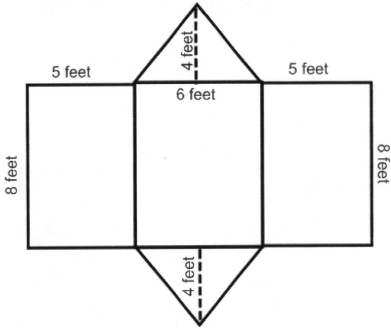

Each triangle has a base of 6 feet and height of 4 feet, so the area of each triangle is $\frac{6 \times 4}{2} = \frac{24}{2} = 12\text{ft}^2$. Each outer rectangle in the net figure has a length of 8 feet and a width of 5 feet, so the area of each of those rectangles is $5 \times 8 = 40\text{ft}^2$. The other rectangle has a length of 8 and a width of 6, so has an area of $6 \times 8 = 48\text{ft}^2$. The total surface area is found by adding the area of all 5 of the separate shapes together: $12 + 12 + 40 + 40 + 48 = 152\text{ft}^2$.

- 8 -

<u>Example problem 2</u>

Draw a net figure of the present below and determine how much wrapping paper will be needed to wrap it.

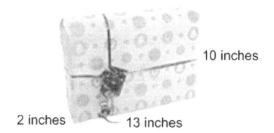

10 inches

2 inches

13 inches

352 square inches of wrapping paper will be needed to wrap the present, which is the surface area of the box. In the net figure below, it is seen that there are two rectangles with dimensions 13in × 2in which each have an area of $13 \times 2 = 26\text{in}^2$, two rectangles with dimensions 10in × 2in which each have an area of $10 \times 2 = 20\text{in}^2$, and two rectangles with dimensions 13in × 10in which each have an area of $13 \times 10 = 130\text{in}^2$. The total surface area is found by adding together the areas of the 6 rectangles: $26 + 26 + 20 + 20 + 130 + 130 = 352\text{in}^2$.

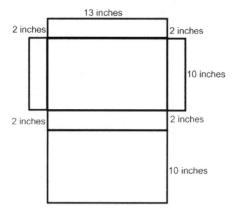

The Number System

Example problem 1

> *Mr. Gordon is Principal at Detroit's largest Middle School and decided to allow students to choose what time they would eat lunch on a given day. To do this he surveyed a group of students and the data is represented in the histogram below. Principal Gordon concluded that he would allow students to eat at their desired lunch time, 11:00-11:30, because the most students wanted to eat during that time. Explain whether or not Principal Gordon's conclusion was justified based on the data in the histogram.*

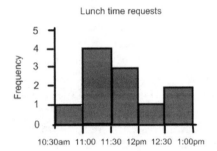

No, Mr. Gordon's conclusion is not justified based on the data given in the histogram. Although the majority of the students he surveyed do want to eat lunch between 11 and 11:30, he only surveyed 11 students. This can be found by adding the frequency of each lunch time period. Surveying a group of 11 students might be a reasonable choice for a very small school, but since Mr. Gordon is the Principal at the largest middle school in Detroit, a sample size of 11 students is not enough to draw justifiable conclusions from. It is possible that the majority of all students will want to each lunch between 11 and 11:30, but Mr. Gordon will need a larger sample size to be able to justify the conclusion that it represents the majority of students' preferences.

<u>Example problem 2</u>

Write an inequality to represent each of the following situations and explain the meaning:
Jim's golf score was 8 under par while Tom's golf score was 2 under par.
Water boils at 212°F and freezes at 32°F.
Yesterday the temperature was −17°F and today the temperature is −21°F.

If we assume 'par' is like zero on the number line, this can be represented by $-8 < -2$, which means that it took Tom a greater number of strokes to finish his golf game, because -2 is greater than -8.

This can be represented by $32° < 212°$, which means that the boiling point of water is warmer than the freezing point of water, because 212° is greater than 32°.

This can be represented by $-21° < -17°$, which means that it was warmer out yesterday because $-17°$ is greater than $-21°$.

<u>Example problem 3</u>

Describe scenarios that might correspond to the following inequalities:
$$-20°F < -5°F$$
$$-\$50 < -\$40$$
$$-6 < -2$$

This represents two different temperatures. One scenario could be that one day it was $-20°F$ in Alaska while the next day it was $-5°F$ there. Since $-5°F$ is greater than $-20°F$, it was warmer the second day.

This represents two amounts of money. One scenario could be that Jenny owes the bank $50 while her friend Susan owes the bank $40. Jenny has a greater debt so therefore a more negative balance, and less money than Susan.

This simply compares two negative integers. One scenario could be that they represent the scores of two golfers. If Max got a golf score of -6 ("six under par") and his friend got a golf score of -2 ("two under par"), then that means it took Max fewer swings to finish the game than it took his friend.

<u>Example problem 4</u>

Represent each scenario below with an absolute value inequality and give one possible solution:
A. Last week Mr. Anderson lost 6 of his cattle to Mad Cow Disease and this week he lost even more.
B. Yesterday Andrus took an elevator from his city street underground 4 stories to the subway. Today Andrus took the same elevator down a fewer number of stories.
C. On Monday Sally withdrew $50 from her bank account and on Tuesday she made a larger withdrawal.

The inequality $|-6| < |x|$ represents the number of cattle Mr. Anderson lost this week, x, compared to the number he lost last week. One possible solution would be $x = -10$, or losing 10 cattle, because $|-6| < |-10|$.

The inequality $|x| < |-4|$ represents how far below ground level Andrus traveled today, x, compared to yesterday. One possible solution would be $x = -1$, or traveling 1 story below ground level, because $|-1| < |-4|$.

The inequality $|-50| < |x|$ represents the amount of Sally's withdrawal on Tuesday, x, compared to her withdrawal Monday. One possible solution would be $x = -100$, or withdrawing $100, because $|-50| < |-100|$.

<u>Example problem 5</u>

Describe a scenario that the following absolute value inequalities could represent:
A. $|-10\ feet| > |-3\ feet|$
B. $|-300\ points| > |-50\ points|$

This inequality could represent the depth of two fish swimming in the ocean. One fish is 10 feet below sea level, or -10 feet, while the other fish is 3 feet below sea level, or -3 feet. The absolute value of -10 is greater than the absolute value of -3, which illustrates the fact the fish swimming 10 feet below sea level is a greater distance from sea level.

This inequality could represent changes in the value of the stock market on two different days. On one day the stock market fell 300 points and the next day the stock market fell 50 points. The absolute value of -300 is greater than the absolute value of -50, illustrating that 300 points is a greater fall than 50 points.

Opposite

The 'opposite' of a number is the number that is the same distance away from zero as the given number but on the other side of zero on a number line. The 'opposite' of a number always has a sign opposite the given number.

The opposite of -4 is 4.
The opposite of 7 is -7.
The opposite of 21 is -21.
The opposite of -10 is 10.
The opposite of 0 is 0. This is because the only number that is the same distance zero is from zero is zero. Zero is neither positive nor negative, so it will not change signs.
The opposite of 13 is -13.
The opposite of -13 is 13.

Number line

<u>Example problem 1</u>
Label a number line with the following values:
   Point A: 2
   Point B: The opposite of 3
   Point C: 0
   Point D: -2
   Point E: The opposite of -5
   Point F: The opposite of -1

The number line below shows the points:

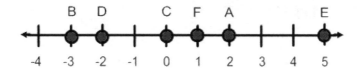

Point A is located at 2 on the number line. Point B is located at -3, which is the opposite of 3. Point C is located at 0. Point D is located at -2. Point E is located at 5, which is the opposite of -5. And Point F is located at 1, which is the opposite of -1.

<u>Example problem 2</u>

Determine the following values, then plot the points on a number line and write an inequality that represents each relation between the points:
5 units to the right of -2
3 units to the left of 1

The number that is 5 units to the right of -2 is 3. The number line below shows these values and it is seen that $3 > -2$ because 3 is located to the right of -2.

The number that is 3 units to the left of 1 is -2. The number line below shows these values and it is seen that $-2 < 1$ because -2 is located to the left of 1.

<u>Example problem 3</u>

Determine the following values, then plot the points on a number line and write an inequality that represents each relation between the points:
1 unit to the left of 1
2 units to the left of -2

A. The number that is 1 unit to the left of 1 is 0. The number line below shows these values and it is seen that $0 < 1$ because 0 is located to the left of 1.

B. The number that is 2 units to the left of -2 is -4. The number line below shows these values and it is seen that $-4 < -2$ because -4 is located to the left of -2.

- 14 -

Absolute value

Absolute Value is how far away a number is from zero on a number line, or the distance between zero and that number. The absolute value of a number is always positive, because distance is positive.

The absolute value of 40 is 40, because it is 40 units away from zero.

The absolute value of -12 is 12 because it is 12 units away from zero.

The absolute value of -25 is 25 because it is 25 units away from zero.

The absolute value of 18 is 18 because it is 18 units away from zero.

The absolute value of -100 is 100 because it is 100 units away from zero.

<u>Example problem 1</u>
Write an absolute value equation to express the following situations:
After the first day of a bike race, Peter is 45 seconds behind the lead racer.
Marla owes her mom $10.
The scuba diver is 20 feet below sea level.

This situation can be represented by $|-45| = 45$. When we say a racer is behind, it actually means that racer's time is longer than the leader's. To catch the leader, then, Peter needs to subtract 45 seconds from his time, and this equation shows that the difference between the times is 45 seconds.

This situation can be represented by $|-10| = 10$. This shows that Marla is in debt $10 to her mom, but Marla does not actually have a negative amount of money so it is expressed as absolute value, which shows that Marla needs to pay $10 to her mom.

This situation can be represented by $|-20| = 20$. This shows that the scuba diver is 20 feet under the measurement we mark as '0' on the earth, sea level. However, the scuba diver is not actually a negative distance from sea level so it is expressed in absolute value, showing the scuba diver is a distance of 20 feet away from sea level.

Division

<u>Example problem</u>

Solve the following division problem:

$$9\overline{)9027}$$

The answer to the problem of 9027 divided by 9 is 1003.

$$
\begin{array}{r}
1003 \\
9\overline{)9027} \\
\underline{9000} \\
0027 \\
\underline{0027} \\
0
\end{array}
$$

Of course, 9 divides into 9 exactly one time, so a 1 is placed on the answer line, and the product of 1 and 9 is placed under the thousands place of the dividend. (The remaining places are zero). 9 does not go into 0, so a 0 is placed on the answer line above 0. Since 9 also does not go into 2, another 0 is placed on the answer line. 9 goes into 27 three times, so a 3 is placed on the answer line above the 7. There is no remainder, because 9 goes into 27 exactly 3 times with nothing left over.

Decimals

<u>Example problem 1</u>

Add the following decimals:

$$
\begin{array}{r}
13.48 \\
+2.5 \\
\end{array}
$$

The answer is 15.98.

$$
\begin{array}{r}
13.48 \\
+2.5 \\
\hline
15.98
\end{array}
$$

It is important to line up the digits correctly which can be done by making sure that the decimal points are lined up vertically, which results in lining up digits that have the same place values. Start by putting a decimal point in the answer line directly below the decimal points in the problem, and then add the digits in the column farthest to the right. There is no digit in 2.5 that lines up with the 8 in 13.48, so 0 is added to 8, and the answer, 8, is brought down below the addition line to the answer. Next, add the 4 and 5, as they are in the same place value (the tenths place in this case); put their sum, 9, in the tenths place of the answer. Adding the digits in the ones place puts a 5 in the ones place of the answer. Finally, the 1 in the tens place in 13.48 isn't added to any digit in 2.5, so the sum of 1 and 0 is put in the tens place of the answer, which makes the final answer 15.98.

Example problem 2
    Subtract the following decimals:
            37.4
            - 5.32

    The answer is 32.08.
            37.4
            - 5.32
            32.08
    It is important to line up the digits correctly which can be done by making
    sure that the decimal points are lined up vertically, which results in lining up
    digits that have the same place values. Start by putting a decimal point in the
    answer line directly below the decimal points in the problem, and then
    subtract the digits in the column farthest to the right, the top minus the
    bottom. Since there is currently no digit above the 2, it is considered a 0, but
    since 2 cannot be subtracted from 0, borrow from the 4, making the 0 a 10
    and making the 4 a 3. Since 2 can now be subtracted from 10, put the
    answer, 8, in the hundredths place of the answer. Now subtract 3
    (remember: it's not a 4 anymore!) from 3, which is 0. In the ones place
    subtract 5 from 7, which is 2. And finally nothing is being subtracted from
    the 3 in the tens place in 37.4, so the 3 is brought down to the answer,
    making the final answer 32.08.

Prime factorization

Prime Factorization is breaking a number down into a list of its prime factors. For example,
the prime factorization of 60 is $2 \times 2 \times 3 \times 5$, because 2, 3, and 5 are all prime numbers and
$2 \times 2 \times 3 \times 5 = 60$. This can be found by first breaking down 60 into any two factors,
perhaps 30 and 2. Since 2 is a prime number, it's already a prime factor, but 30 needs to be
broken down into factors. 30 can be broken into 2 and 15, 3 and 10, or 6 and 5, but it does
not matter which we use. If 3 and 10 are used, the factorization of 60 is $2 \times 3 \times 10$. Since 2
and 3 are prime but 10 is not, we have to break 10 down into 2 and 5, which now makes the
factorization of $60 = 2 \times 3 \times 2 \times 5$. This is the prime factorization of 60 because these
numbers are all prime. To report the answer in proper form put the numbers in order from
least to greatest: the final answer for the prime factorization of 60 is $2 \times 2 \times 3 \times 5$.

Greatest common factor

The greatest common factor is the greatest number that all numbers in a set are evenly
divisible by. For example, the Greatest Common Factor of 36 and 48 is 12. One way to find
this is by simply listing all the factors of 36 and 48; the common factors of 36 and 48 are 1,
2, 3, 4, 6, and 12, and 12 is the greatest of these. This can also be found using the prime
factorization of both 36 and 48. The prime factorization of 36 is $2 \times 2 \times 3 \times 3$, and the
prime factorization of 48 is $2 \times 2 \times 2 \times 2 \times 3$. Find how many of each prime factor these
factorizations have in common: both factorizations have two 2's and one 3, so the Greatest
Common Factor of 36 and 48 must be $2 \times 2 \times 3$, which equals 12.

<u>Examples</u>

The following sums can be expressed by factoring out a common factor:
15 + 21
16 + 20
50 + 80
27 + 63
6 + 52
18 + 66

'15 + 21' = 3(5 + 7)
'16 + 20' = 4(4 + 5)
'50 + 80' = 10(5 + 8)
'27 + 63' = 9(3 + 7)
'6 + 52' = 2(3 + 26)
'18 + 66' = 6(3 + 11)

These answers cannot be factored any further because there are no common factors left between the numbers inside the parentheses. In other words, the number that was factored out of each pair of numbers is that pair's greatest common factor.

Least common multiple

The least common multiple is the smallest number that is evenly divisible by all numbers in a given set. For example, the least common multiple of 6 and 8 is 24. One way to find this is to list the common multiples of 6 and 8, 24, 48, 72, ...etc, and the least of these is 24. This can also be found using the prime factorization of both 6 and 8. The prime factorization of 6 is 2×3, and the prime factorization of 8 is $2 \times 2 \times 2$. For each factor, count the number of times it occurs in each factorization. Find the greatest number of times each factor shows up, and multiply each factor that many times. Since 2 shows up three times in 8's factorization, and 3 shows up once in 6's prime factorization, multiply $2 \times 2 \times 2 \times 3$, which equals 24.

Highest and lowest temperature

<u>Example problem</u>

At 1am in Anchorage, Alaska, it was -17°outside. The temperature fell a total of 10 degrees by sunrise, and then rose steadily a total of 35 degrees until 1pm, when the highest temperature of the day occurred. Find the lowest temperature during the night and the warmest temperature of the day.

The lowest temperature during the night was -27° and the warmest temperature of the day was 8°. Since the temperature falls 10° from -17°, subtract 10 from -17: -17 -10 = -27, and the lowest temperature was -27°. From this lowest temperature it rises a total 35° which brings the thermometer up to 8° because -27 + 35 = 8. This can be thought of in two ways: first, because of the commutative property, -27 + 35 = 35 + -27, which is the same as 35 – 27, which equals 8. The other way is to recognize that the temperature must rise 27 degrees from -27° to get to 0°, but we know it rises another 8°, because the difference between 35 and 27 is 8.

Addition and subtraction with positives and negatives

<u>Example problem 1</u>

On Monday of last week, Molly's credit card had a balance of $50 owing on it. Throughout the week Molly made new charges on her credit card when she spent $75 at the grocery store on Tuesday, $30 on a haircut on Wednesday, and $15 at the movies on Friday. On Saturday she made a payment of $200 to her credit card and then on Sunday made another charge of $40 to buy new shoes. Determine whether Molly's credit card has a balance on Sunday night, and if so, how much it is.

Molly's credit card has a balance of $10 on Sunday night. This can be found by subtracting Molly's charges and adding her payment to her balance. A charge on a credit card, or balance, is a negative number because it is owed to the credit card company. A payment on the card gives the company money they are owed, so it is a positive number added to the balance to make that balance *less* negative. In Molly's case, she starts the week with a $50 balance, which is like starting with -50. The three charges on Tuesday, Wednesday, and Friday need to be subtracted from this, to get $-50 - 75 - 30 - 15 = -170$. When Molly makes a payment of $200, then, she only owed $170 on her credit card, so that -170 + 200 = positive 30. (Positive balances are money the company owes to Molly!) After that she makes another charge of $40, which is subtracted from 30 to get a final amount of -10. This means that at the end of the week Molly owes her credit card company $10, and we say her credit card has a balance of $10.

- 19 -

<u>Example problem 2</u>

A helicopter is flying directly above a submarine. The submarine travels to 600 feet below sea level, while the helicopter reaches its flying height of 1050 feet. Find how far away the submarine and helicopter are from each other.

The helicopter and submarine are 1650 feet apart. This is found by adding their distances to sea level, because we can think of sea level as a value of zero in this situation. The helicopter is 1050 feet above sea level, which is like +1050, and its distance to sea level, 0, is 1050 feet. The submarine is 600 feet below sea level, which is like -600, and the distance from the submarine to sea level is 600 feet. The total distance between the helicopter and submarine, then, is 1050 + 600 = 1650 feet.

Coordinate plane

<u>Four quadrants and the range of x and y-values</u>
The four quadrants in a coordinate plane are called Quadrant I, Quadrant II, Quadrant III, and Quadrant IV. Quadrant I is the upper right quadrant of the plane and contains ordered pairs where $x > 0$ and $y > 0$. Quadrant II is the upper left quadrant of the plane and contains ordered pairs where $x < 0$ and $y > 0$. Quadrant III is the lower left quadrant of the plane and contains ordered pairs where $x < 0$ and $y < 0$. Quadrant IV is the lower right quadrant of the plane and contains ordered pairs where $x > 0$ and $y < 0$. The coordinate plane below shows the four quadrants:

<u>Example problem 1</u>

Plot the data in the table below on a coordinate plane and find the value of y when $x = 1$.

X	Y
-4	-1
-2	1
0	3
2	5

Pairs of values (x, y) in the table are plotted on the coordinate plane below:

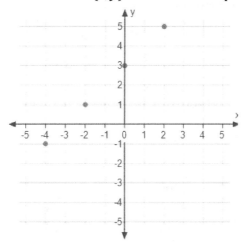

The value of y is 4 when $x = 1$. This can be found by looking at the graph or the table to determine what the pattern of the data is and where the point would lie when $x = 1$. The pattern in the graph and table is that y increases at a rate of 1 vertically for every 1 horizontally; in other words, for every time x increases by 1, y increases by 1 also. It can then be determined that since the y-value was 3 when the x-value was 0, the y-value will be 4 when the x-value is 1.

<u>Example problem 2</u>

Plot the following points in a coordinate plane and describe each point's location:

    Point A: (5, 0)
    Point B: (-2, 2)
    Point C: (-3, -1)
    Point D: (3, 1)
    Point E: (0, 0)
    Point F: (0, -4)
    Point G: (2, -3)

The graph below shows the location of the points:

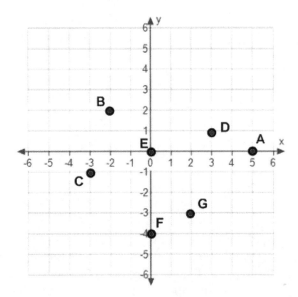

Point A is located on the $x-axis$, 5 units to the right of the origin. Point B is located in Quadrant II, 2 units to the left of the origin and 2 units up. Point C is located in Quadrant III, 3 units to the left of the origin and 1 unit down. Point D is located in Quadrant I, 3 units to the right of the origin and 1 unit up. Point E is located at the origin. Point F is located on the $y-axis$, 4 units down from the origin. Point G is located in Quadrant IV, 2 units to the right of the origin and 3 units down.

<u>Example problem 3</u>

Find the perimeter of the rectangle in the coordinate plane below using the values of the coordinates of the vertices:

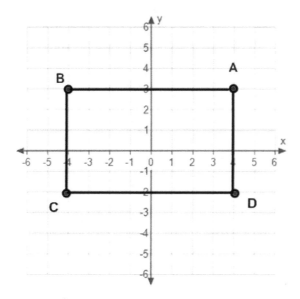

The perimeter of the rectangle is 26 units. This can be found by first finding the ordered pairs of each vertex of the rectangle, which are A= (4, 3), B= (-4, 3), C= (-4, -2), and D= (4, -2), and then using these to find the lengths of the four sides of the rectangle. Since each consecutive pair of vertices share either the same $x -$ coordinate or $y -$ coordinate, it is only necessary to consider the coordinates that are different in value. The distances from A to B and from C to D are each 8, which can be found by finding the distance between their $x -$ coordinates. The distance between 4 and -4 is 8, because 4 is 4 units away from zero and -4 is also 4 units away from zero which gives a total length of $4 + 4 = 8$. The distance from B to C and from D to A are each 5, which can be found by finding the distance between their $y -$ coordinates. The distance between 3 and -2 is 5, because 3 is 3 units away from zero and -2 is 2 units away from zero which gives a total length of $3 + 2 = 5$. Therefore the total perimeter of the rectangle is $8 + 8 + 5 + 5 = 26$ units.

Example problem 4

Find the remaining ordered pairs of the vertices of a square in the coordinate plane below if one side length of the square is 5 units and it has a vertex in each quadrant.

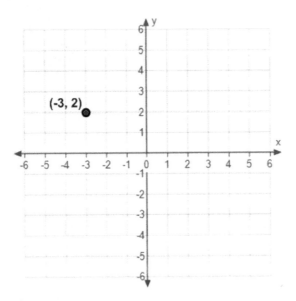

The remaining vertices have the ordered pairs of (-3, -3), (2, -3), and (2, 2). This is found by first figuring out what point in Quadrant III is 5 units away from the given point. It will have the same x −coordinate, so the value of y needs to be 5 units away from 2. Going 2 units away from 2 gets to 0, and then 3 more units must be traveled, getting to the point (-3, -3). Then figure out what point in Quadrant IV is 5 units away from (-3, -3). It will have the same y −coordinate, so the value of x needs to be 5 units away from -3. Going 3 units to the right of -3 gets to 0, and then 2 more units must be traveled, getting to the point (2, -3). Finally figure out what point in Quadrant I is 5 units away from (2, -3). It will have the same x −coordinate as the point in Quadrant IV, and the same y-coordinate as the point in Quadrant II, so the point must be (2, 2). This can be verified: the value of y needs to be 5 units away from -3. Going 3 units away from -3 gets to 0, and then 2 more units must be traveled, getting to the point (2, 2).

<u>Example problem 5</u>

Platt Middle School was designed using a coordinate grid with each unit of measure representing 1 block. In the school, the library is located at (1, 4), the cafeteria is located at (-3, 4) and the gym is located at (1, -2). Plot these points on a coordinate grid and find the shortest distance a student needs to walk to get from gym class to the library and then to lunch.

The student will need to walk 10 blocks. This can be found by first finding the distance from the gym at (1, -2) to the library at (1, 4), and then the library to the cafeteria at (-3, 4). To get from the gym to the library the student will need to walk along a straight path along the x-coordinate of 1, from y-coordinates -2 to 4. The distance -2 is from 0 is 2, and the distance 4 is from 0 is 4. Therefore, the student must walk $2 + 4 = 6$ blocks from the gym to the library. Then the student will walk in a straight path along the y-coordinate of 4 from x-coordinates 1 to -3. The distance 1 is from 0 is 1, and the distance -3 is from 0 is 3. Therefore, the student must walk $1 + 3 = 4$ blocks from the library to lunch in the cafeteria. Thus, the student must walk a total of $6 + 4 = 10$ blocks to get from the gym to the library and then to lunch. The graph below shows the location of the places in the school and the student's path:

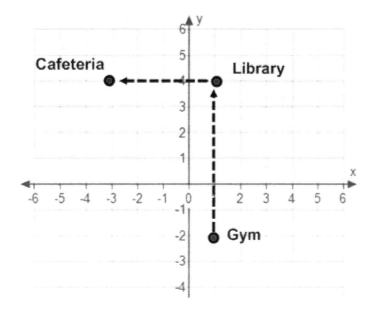

- 25 -

<u>Example problem 6</u>

The downtown area of Cannonville has streets that follow a coordinate grid. The mayor is planning a parade through downtown and the city council has limited the length of the parade to 16 blocks. The mayor wants the parade to travel from the Zoo at (-5, -4) to the Park at (-3, -4), to the Bakery at (-3, 1), to the Library at (-1, 1), to the Post Office at (-1, -1), to City Hall at (2, -1), and ending at the Town Square at (2, 2). Plot this proposed route of the parade on a coordinate plane and determine if it will fit the requirement of the city council.

The distance of the proposed parade is 17 blocks so it will not make the 16 block requirement from the city council. This distance can be found by determining the distance between each pair of consecutive parade locations. Since each pair of consecutive locations share either an x or y −coordinate, the distance is found by calculating the distance between the different coordinates. When finding the distance between coordinates of opposite signs, first find the absolute value of each, which gives the distance of each from 0, and add them together. The distances are: **1.** Zoo to Park is 2 blocks, which is the distance between x −coordinates -5 and -3. **2.** Park to Bakery is 5 blocks, which is the distance between y-coordinates -4 and 1 because $|-4| + |1| = 5$. **3.** Bakery to the Library is 2 blocks, which is the distance between x −coordinates -3 and -1. **4.** Library to Post Office is 2 blocks, which is the distance between y-coordinates 1 and -1 because $|-1| + |1| = 2$. **5.** Post Office to City Hall is 3 blocks, which is the distance between x-coordinates -1 and 2 because $|-1| + |2| = 3$. **6.** City Hall to Town Square is 3 blocks, which is the distance between y-coordinates -1 and 2 because $|-1| + |2| = 3$. **7.** The total distance is then $2 + 5 + 2 + 2 + 3 + 3 = 17$.

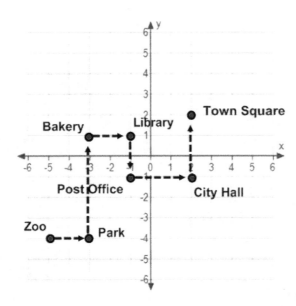

- 26 -

Reflections

<u>Example problem 1</u>

Label the following points and their indicated reflections in a coordinate plane and give the coordinates of the reflections:
Point A: (4, 3) reflected across the $x - axis$
Point B: (1, 2) reflected across the $y - axis$
Point C: (-2, -5) reflected across the $y - axis$
Point D: (3, 1) reflected across the $x - axis$ and then the $y - axis$

The graph below shows the points and their reflections:
The reflection of Point A is labeled as A' and has coordinates (4, -3). Because it is reflected across the $x - axis$, the $y - value$ changes in sign.
The reflection of Point B is labeled as B' and has coordinates (-1, 2). Because it is reflected across the $y - axis$, the $x - value$ changes in sign.
The reflection of Point C is labeled as C' and has coordinates (2, -5). Because it is reflected across the $y - axis$, the $x - value$ changes in sign.
The reflection of Point D is labeled as D' and has coordinates (-3, -1). Because it is reflected across both the x and $y - axes$, both the x and $y - values$ change in sign.

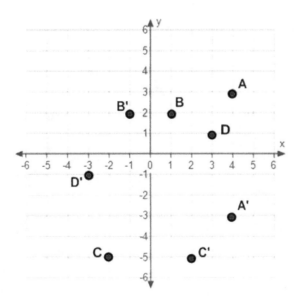

- 27 -

<u>Example problem 2</u>

Identify the reflections that produce the second of each pair from the first of each pair:
(2, 6) and (-2, 6)
(-4, 0) and (4, 0)
(-1, -1) and (-1, 1)
(5, -7) and (-5, 7)

The reflection from (2, 6) to (-2, 6) is a reflection across the $y-axis$. This is because the $x-value$ has changed in sign.

The reflection from (-4, 0) to (4, 0) is a reflection across the $y-axis$. This is because the $x-value$ has changed in sign.

The reflection from (-1, -1) to (-1, 1) is a reflection across the $x-axis$. This is because the $y-value$ has changed in sign.

The reflection from (5, -7) to (-5, 7) is a reflection across both the x and $y-axis$. This is because both the x and $y-values$ have changed in sign.

Fractions

<u>Example problem 1</u>

You and your best friend plan to split the remaining amount of a large pizza. If there is $\frac{3}{4}$ of the pizza left, find what fraction of the original pizza each of you will get and represent the solution with a diagram.

You each get $\frac{3}{8}$ of the original pizza. This is found by dividing $\frac{3}{4}$ by 2. When dividing with fractions, dividing by a number is the same as multiplying by the reciprocal of that number, so that $\frac{3}{4} \div 2 = \frac{3}{4} \times \frac{1}{2}$.

Multiply the numerators together to obtain the numerator of the product, and multiply the denominators to get the denominator of the product: $\frac{3}{4} \times \frac{1}{2} = \frac{3}{8}$. This division problem can be represented by the diagram shown.

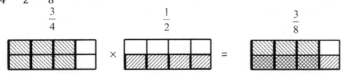

In the first part of the diagram, $\frac{3}{4}$ of the squares are shaded. In the second diagram, $\frac{1}{2}$ of the squares are shaded. Any squares that are shaded in both diagrams will be the answer. The overlap of the two diagrams shows that 3 of the 8 squares overlap, or $\frac{3}{8}$ of the whole. Or, consider dividing the first diagram, which has 6 out of the 8 squares shaded, by two. This would mean taking away half of the shaded squares, which would also result in 3 of the 8 squares shaded, or an answer of $\frac{3}{8}$.

- 28 -

<u>Example problem 2</u>

Ms. Redding is going to frame two new rectangular posters she bought while on vacation. Before placing the order for the frames she needs to know the dimensions of each poster. When she bought the posters she was told that the area of each is $2/3$ square yards, the width of one is $3/4$ yards and the width of the other is $1/2$ yard. Find the length of each poster.

The lengths of the two posters are $8/9$ yards and $1\,1/3$ yards, respectively. Because $Area = length \times width$ for any rectangle, then $l = \frac{A}{w}$. To solve for the length of each rectangle, divide the area ($2/3$ square yards) by each width. When dividing by a fraction you must multiply by the reciprocal of that fraction.

For the first poster, $l = \frac{2}{3} \div \frac{3}{4} = \frac{2}{3} \times \frac{4}{3} = \frac{8}{9}$, and the length of the first poster is $8/9$ yards. For the second poster, $l = \frac{2}{3} \div \frac{1}{2} = \frac{2}{3} \times \frac{2}{1} = \frac{4}{3} = 1\,1/3$, and the length of the second poster is $1\,1/3$ yards.

Important terms

Integer - An integer is any whole number, including 0 and all the negative whole numbers as well. The values $-100, -12, -1, 4,$ and 13 are all integers because they are all whole numbers, whether positive or negative. The values -2.65, $\frac{1}{3}$, and $\sqrt{6}$ are not integers because they are not whole numbers.

Rational number - A rational number is any number that can be expressed as a fraction. Equivalently, a rational number is any number that can be expressed as a terminating or repeating decimal. Rational numbers can be both positive and negative. The values $-\frac{2}{5}$ and 3 are rational numbers because $-\frac{2}{5}$ is a fraction and 3 can be expressed as a fraction as $\frac{3}{1}$. Any integer can be expressed as a fraction as itself over 1, so all integers are also rational numbers. The values $\sqrt{8}$ and π are not rational numbers (they are called 'irrational numbers') because they cannot be expressed as a fraction. These numbers are decimals that continue on without ending or repeating.

Prime number - A prime number is a number that is only evenly divisible by 1 and itself.

Prime factor - A prime factor is a prime number that divides evenly into another number. For example, 3 is a prime factor of 21, because 3 is a prime number and 21 is evenly divisible by 3.

Least common multiple - The least common multiple is the smallest number that is evenly divisible by all numbers in a given set.

Greatest common factor - The greatest common factor is the greatest number that all numbers in a set are evenly divisible by.

Ratios and Proportional Relationships

Ratio

A ratio is a direct comparison of two parts of a whole. This is not the same as comparing each part to the whole, as in the case of fractions. For example, for every 3 girls in Maggie's class there are 5 boys. The ratio of girls to boys is a direct comparison of the number of girls and boys, and is therefore 3:5. (Note how this is different from a fraction: 3/8 of the students in Maggie's class are girls, which relates the number of one part, girls, to the whole, students.) Any ratio can be written in three ways: with a colon, as a fraction, or with the word "to". For example, the ratio of girls to boys in Maggie's class can be written as either "3:5", "$\frac{3}{5}$", or "3 to 5". All three ways are read as "three to five".

The following shows how ratios can describe various situations:

- Every car in the parking lot has four wheels. - "Every car in the parking lot has four wheels," means the ratio of cars to wheels is 1:4, because for every one car there are four wheels.
- There are two eyes on every face. - "There are two eyes on every face," means the ratio of eyes to faces is 2:1, because for every two eyes there is one face.
- Every full deck of cards has four aces. - "Every full deck of cards has four aces," means either that the ratio of decks to aces is 1:4, because for each deck there are four aces, or that the ratio of cards to aces is 52:4, because for every set of 52 cards (1 deck), there are 4 aces.
- A recipe calls for two cups of flour for every two dozen cookies. - "A recipe calls for two cups of flour for every two dozen cookies," means the ratio of cups of flour to cookies is 2:24, because for every two cups of flour used 24 (two dozen) cookies will be made.

Unit rate

Unit rate expresses a quantity of one thing in terms of one unit of another. For example, if you travel 30 miles every two hours, a unit rate expresses this comparison in terms of one hour: in one hour you travel 15 miles, so your unit rate is 15 miles per hour. Other examples are how much one ounce of food costs (price per ounce), or figuring out how much one egg costs out of the dozen (price per 1 egg, instead of price per 12 eggs). The denominator of a unit rate is always 1. Unit rates are used to compare different situations to solve problems. For example, to make sure you get the best deal when deciding which kind of soda to buy, you can find the unit rate of each. If Soda #1 costs $1.50 for a 1-liter bottle, and soda #2 costs $2.75 for a 2-liter bottle, it would be a better deal to buy Soda #2, because its unit rate is only $1.375 per 1-liter, which is cheaper than Soda #1. Unit rates can also help determine the length of time a given event will take. For example, if you can paint 2 rooms in 4.5 hours, you can determine how long it will take you to paint 5 rooms by solving for the unit rate per room and then multiplying that by 5.

Example problem 1

> *At the store you see two different bags of candy for sale. Bag A has 32 pieces of candy in it and costs $2.10. Bag B has 50 pieces of candy in it and costs $3.50. Find the unit cost per one piece of candy from each bag and determine which is the better deal.*

One piece of candy in Bag A costs about $0.065, or 6.5 cents. This can be found be taking the total price, $2.10, and dividing it by the number of pieces of candy, 32, to determine the cost for one piece of candy: $\frac{2.10}{32} = 0.06562$, or about $0.065. One piece of candy in Bag B costs $0.07, or 7 cents. This can be found in the same way, dividing the total cost, $3.50, by the number of pieces of candy, 50: $\frac{3.5}{50} = 0.07$, or $0.07. Since a piece of candy in Bag B is slightly more expensive, it is the better deal to buy Bag A.

Example problem 2

> *You decide to bake oatmeal cookies for a bake sale. Your recipe calls for 5 cups of flour, 2 cups of sugar, 1 cup of butter, and 3 cups of oats. However, you only have 1 cup of oats. You decide to make as many cookies as you can with the 1 cup of oats that you have. Find how much of each ingredient you will need to make that many cookies.*

You will need to use $1\,^2/_3$ cups of flour, $^2/_3$ cup of sugar, and $^1/_3$ cup of butter. These can be found by finding the unit rate of each per 1 cup of oats. If there are 5 cups of flour needed for every 3 cups of oats, then $\frac{5}{3} = 1\,^2/_3$ cups of flour needed for every 1 cup of oats. Similarly, if there needs to be 2 cups of sugar for every 3 cups of oats, then there needs to be $^2/_3$ cup of sugar for every 1 cup of oats. And finally, if there is 1 cup of butter needed for every 3 cups of oats, then there will need to be $^1/_3$ cup of butter for every 1 cup of oats.

Example problem 3

Janice made $40 during the first 5 hours she spent babysitting. She will continue to earn money at this rate until she finishes babysitting in 3 more hours. Find how much money Janice earned babysitting and how much she earns per hour.

Janice will earn $64 babysitting in her 8 total hours (adding the first 5 hours to the remaining 3 gives the 8 hour total). This can be found by setting up a proportion comparing money earned to babysitting hours. Since she earns $40 for 5 hours and since the rate is constant, she will earn a proportional amount in 8 hours: $\frac{40}{5} = \frac{x}{8}$. Cross-multiplying will yield $5x = 320$, and division by 5 shows that $x = 64$.

Janice earns $8 per hour. This can be found by taking her total amount earned, $64, and dividing it by the total number of hours worked, 8. Since $\frac{64}{8} = 8$, Janice makes $8 in one hour. This can also be found by finding the unit rate, money earned per hour: $\frac{64}{8} = \frac{x}{1}$. Since cross-multiplying yields $8x = 64$, and division by 8 shows that $x = 8$, Janice earns $8 per hour.

Example problem 4

The McDonalds are taking a family road trip, driving 300 miles to their cabin. It took them 2 hours to drive the first 120 miles. They will drive at the same speed all the way to their cabin. Find the speed at which the McDonalds are driving and how much longer it will take them to get to their cabin.

The McDonalds are driving 60 miles per hour. This can be found by setting up a proportion to find the unit rate, the number of miles they drive per one hour: $\frac{120}{2} = \frac{x}{1}$. Cross-multiplying yields $2x = 120$ and division by 2 shows that $x = 60$.

Since the McDonalds will drive this same speed, it will take them another 3 hours to get to their cabin. This can be found by first finding how many miles the McDonalds have left to drive, which is 300 – 120 = 180. The McDonalds are driving at 60 miles per hour, so a proportion can be set up to determine how many hours it will take them to drive 180 miles: $\frac{180}{x} = \frac{60}{1}$. Cross-multiplying yields $60x = 180$, and division by 60 shows that $x = 3$. This can also be found by using the formula $D = r \times t$ (or $Distance = rate \times time$), where $180 = 60 \times t$, and division by 60 shows that $t = 3$.

<u>Example problem 5</u>

It takes Andy 10 minutes to read 6 pages of his book. He has already read 150 pages in his book that is 210 pages long. Find how long it takes Andy to read 1 page and also find how long it will take him to finish his book if he continues to read at the same speed.

It takes Andy 1 minute and 40 seconds to read one page in his book. This can be found by finding the unit rate per one page, by dividing the total time it takes him to read 6 pages by 6. Since it takes him 10 minutes to read 6 pages, $\frac{10}{6} = 1\,{}^2/_3$ minutes, which is 1 minute and 40 seconds.

It will take Andy another 100 minutes, or 1 hour and 40 minutes to finish his book. This can be found by first figuring out how many pages Andy has left to read, which is 210-150 = 60. Since it is now known that it takes him $1\,{}^2/_3$ minutes to read each page, then that rate must be multiplied by however many pages he has left to read (60) to find the time he'll need: $60 \times 1\,{}^2/_3 = 100$, so it will take him 100 minutes, or 1 hour and 40 minutes, to read the rest of his book.

<u>Example problem 6</u>

Find the unit rate in the situations given:
A. Pizza Place is offering a deal for $40 for 8 pizzas. What is the cost of each pizza?
B. The ratio of flight attendants to airplanes is 42:14. How many flight attendants are on each airplane?
C. Milo has a pledge of $100 for the 25 mile walk-a-thon. How much will Milo earn for each mile?
D. It takes the cleaning service 8 hours to clean 20 garages. How long does it take to clean 1 garage?

A. The unit rate is $5 per pizza. This is found by $\frac{\$40}{8} = \$5$.

B. The unit ratio is 3:1 which means there are 3 flight attendants for each airplane. This is found by $\frac{42}{14} = 3$.

C. The unit rate is $4 per mile. This is found by $\frac{\$100}{25} = \$4$.

D. The unit rate is 0.4 hours, or 24 minutes, to clean one garage. This is found by $\frac{8\ hours}{20} = 0.4$ hours. This can be converted to minutes multiplying by a conversion factor: $0.4\ hours \times \frac{60\ minutes}{1\ hour} = 24\ minutes$.

Percent

Percent is one way of expressing what portion something is out of a whole. You can think of it like dividing the whole into 100 equal parts, called percents. The whole, all 100 parts, is called 100% (read as "one hundred percent"). Half of the whole is half (50) of the parts, so we say it is 50%, and so on. (Percent compares one quantity to another; sometimes neither number is necessarily 'whole' or 'all' of something.) To find what percent one number is of another, divide the first by the second, and multiply the answer by 100. For example, we can

- 33 -

use percent to compare a part to a whole by asking how much money someone spends on their housing payment each month out of his or her total amount of money that month. If someone earns $2000 every month and spends $800 of that on their housing payment, then that person spends $\frac{800}{2000} \times (100) = 0.4 \times 100 = 40\%$ of his or her income on housing payments. Another example showing how percent can simply relate two numbers is comparing your age to your mother's age. If you are 12 years old and your mother is 40 years old, then you are $\frac{12}{40} \times 100 = 0.3 \times 100 = 30\%$ of her age.

Example problem 1

> *Johnny got 80% of the questions correct on his math test. Find how many questions Johnny answered correctly if the test had 75 questions on it. Also, find what Johnny's new score would be if he was able to earn an extra 10% of his original score by doing corrections on the questions he missed.*

Johnny got 60 questions correct. To find this, set up the percent calculation, leaving the number Johnny got right as x: $(\frac{x}{75} \times 100 = 80\%$. Multiply both sides by 75 and then divide both sides by 100 to solve for $x = \frac{80 \times 75}{100} = 60$. We say we are finding 80% of 75, which we now know means simply multiplying 75 by 0.80, which is 60.

Johnny's new score would be $^{66}/_{75}$, which is a score of 88%. This can be found in two ways. One is finding what number of questions is 10% of Johnny's original number right, or 10% of 60, which is 6 questions. If Johnny gets those 6 questions added back to his score, he would then have a total of 66 questions correct out of 75, which is $\frac{66}{75}$, which is 0.88, or 88%. The other way is by finding 10% of Johnny's original score of 80% and adding that to his original score: 10% of 80% = 0.10 × 80% = 8%, and 80% + 8% = 88%.

Example problem 2

> *A sweater at a local department store is on sale for $33. Find the original price of the sweater if it is marked 40% off the original price.*

The sweater was originally $55. To find this, set up a proportion to determine what number 33 is 60% of. We use 60% because if the sweater is 40% *off* we *subtracted* 40% from the price, so we have 60% *left*. The proportion will compare the percent over 100 to 33 over the original price: $\frac{60}{100} = \frac{33}{x}$. Cross-multiplying yields $60x = 3300$, and division by 60 shows that $x = 55$.

Greater or equal to

<u>Examples</u>

For each situation listed below, determine which quantity is greater or if they are equal:
3 yards and 20 feet
70 minutes and 1 hour
188 pennies and 2 dollars
2 feet and 24 inches
1 kilometer and 100 meters

20 feet is greater. Since there are 3 feet in each yard, there are 9 feet in 3 yards, and 20 feet is greater than 9 feet.

70 minutes is greater, since there are only 60 minutes in one hour.

2 dollars is greater. Since there are 100 pennies in each dollar, there are 200 pennies in 2 dollars, which is greater than 188 pennies.

These quantities are equal, since there are 12 inches in each foot, and therefore 24 inches in 2 feet.

1 kilometer is greater, because in each kilometer there are 1000 meters, which is greater than 100 meters.

Conversions

<u>Example problem 1</u>

Tony is going to buy new carpet for two rooms in his house. One room is
$12\ feet \times 12\ feet$, *and the other is* $10\ feet \times 18\ feet$. *The carpet Tony wants to buy is on sale for $10 per square yard. How much will Tony pay for the amount of carpet he needs for both rooms?*

Tony will pay $360 for his carpet. First figure out how much carpet Tony needs to buy in square yards and then multiply that by $10 per square yard.

Since Tony's room dimensions are in feet, they must first be converted to yards. The first room is 12 feet × 12 feet, and since there are 3 feet in each yard, that room is 4 yards × 4 yards (because $^{12}/_3 = 4$). Similarly, the room that is 10 feet × 18 feet measures $3\ ^1/_3$ yards × 6 yards (because $^{10}/_3 = 3\ ^1/_3$, and $^{18}/_3 = 6$). So, the total square yardage of Tony's rooms is $4 \times 4 = 16$ square yards, plus $3\ ^1/_3 \times 6 = 20$ square yards, or $16 + 20 = 36$ square yards. Since the carpet costs $10 per square yard, then the total cost is $\$10 \times 36 = \$360$.

Example problem 2

Tyson is driving home from work. He is driving 45 miles per hour and is 10 miles away from home. Find how many minutes it will take Tyson to get the rest of the way home if he continues to drive at the same speed.

It will take Tyson $13\,^1/_3$ minutes to get home. Convert Tyson's speed to miles per minute, using a conversion factor of 60 minutes in 1 hour: $\frac{45\ miles}{1\ hour} \times \frac{1\ hour}{60\ minutes} = 0.75\ miles/minute.$ (The 'hours' units cancel and the answer is then in 'miles per minute'.) Because $distance = rate \times time$, $\frac{distance}{rate} = time.$ Therefore, if Tyson has 10 miles left to go, dividing that by 0.75 miles per minute finds how many minutes it will take Tyson to get home. $\frac{10}{0.75} = 13\,^1/_3,$ so it will take Tyson $13\,^1/_3$ minutes to get home.

Example problem 3

When Mrs. Smith turned 50 years old she wanted to figure out how many minutes she had been alive. She determined that she had been alive for 25,000,000 minutes. Is she correct?

No, Mrs. Smith is not correct. She has been alive for 26,280,000 minutes. This is found by converting 50 years into minutes, using conversion factors from years to days to hours to minutes: $50\ years \times \frac{365\ days}{1\ year} \times \frac{24\ hours}{1\ day} \times \frac{60\ minutes}{1\ hour} = 26{,}280{,}000$ minutes. The first multiplication operation will give 18,250, which is how many days Mrs. Smith has been alive (the 'years' units cancel). Multiplying that by $\frac{24\ hours}{1\ day}$ will cancel the 'days' units and yield 438,000 hours. Finally, multiplying that by $\frac{60\ minutes}{1\ hour}$ will cancel the 'hours' units and leave an answer of 26,280,000 minutes.

Proportions

<u>Example problem 1</u>

Using the table below, find the values of a and b.

Gallons of Gas	Price in Dollars
2	a
5	20
b	32
9	36

The value of a is 8 and the value of b is also 8. They can both be found by setting up proportions. To find the value of a, a proportion can be set up comparing 2 and a with the values in the second row, 5 and 20: $\frac{2}{a} = \frac{5}{20}$. Cross multiplying yields $40 = 5a$, and division by 5 shows that $a = 8$.

To find the value of b, another proportion can be set up, comparing b and 32 with any other pair of data in the table. Using 9 and 36 yields the proportion $\frac{b}{32} = \frac{9}{36}$, and cross multiplying yields $36b = 288$. Division by 36 shows that $b = 8$.

<u>Example problem 2</u>

Using the tables comparing Janaya's and Tim's running speeds, decide who will win a race that is 100 meters long.

Janaya

Distance	Time
10m	1.4 seconds
45m	6.3 seconds
85m	11.9 seconds

Tim

Distance	Time
12m	1.8 seconds
50m	7.5 seconds
85m	11.25 seconds

Janaya will win a 100m race against Tim, because Janaya will run 100m in 14 seconds, and Tim will run 100m in 15 seconds. Set up proportions to solve for what each runner's time will be for a 100m distance. To solve for Janaya's time, we can compare 100m with the unknown time, x, to any other pair of data in her table. If we use 10m and 1.4 seconds, the proportion $\frac{10}{1.4} = \frac{100}{x}$ yields $10x = 140$ after cross-multiplication and division by 10 yields $x = 14$. To solve for Tim's time, we can compare 100m with his unknown time, y, to any other pair of data in his table. If we use 50m and 7.5 seconds, the proportion $\frac{50}{7.5} = \frac{100}{y}$ will give $50y = 750$ and division by 50 will give $y = 15$. Since it will take Tim 1 second longer, Janaya will win.

Statistics and Probability

Mean, median, and mode

Example problem 1

Define the following terms and find each for the data listed below:
Mean
Median
Mode
22, 17, 14, 15, 11, 20, 16, 15, 12, 14, 14

The *Mean* is the average of a set of data. This is found by dividing the sum of the data values by the number of values there are. The mean of the given data is 15.455, which is found by dividing the sum of the data by 11 because there are 11 terms in the data: $\frac{22+17+14+15+11+20+16+15+12+14+14}{11} = 15.455$.

The *Median* is the middle number in a set of data, and can be found by listing the data in order from least to greatest and crossing one off on either end until the middle is reached. If there are two middle terms the average of them is the median of the data. The median of the given data is 15:
$11, 12, 14, 14, 14, 15, 15, 16, 17, 20, 22$.

The *mode* is the value in a set of data that occurs the most often. In the given data the mode is 14, because that value occurs 3 times while all other values are only in the list 1 or 2 times.

Example problem 2

The following are the test scores Michaela earned in math class. Her teacher is deciding whether the mean or the median score would best represent Michaela's final grade in math. Based on the data, determine if the teacher should use the mean or the median.
Michaela's Test Scores
50, 55, 58, 58, 90, 92, 99

Michaela's teacher should use the mean test score. The mean test score is found by dividing the sum of the data values by how many there are. The mean of Michaela's test scores is $\frac{50+55+58+58+90+92+99}{7} = \frac{502}{7} = 71.7$. The median of Michaela's test scores is the number in the middle, which is 58: $50, 55, 58, 58, 90, 92, 99$. Since Michaela appears to have improved, it is more reasonable for her to have a passing grade of 71.7% than a failing grade at 58%. Therefore the mean better represents this data.

Example problem 3

You want to go to the ballpark to buy tickets to a baseball game. To ensure that you are able to get tickets you will need to get in the line that has the least waiting time. At the ballpark there are two lines: Red and Blue. You surveyed your friends who have bought tickets in the past to find their wait times. Analyze the data you collected below, decide which line you should wait in to purchase tickets. Time (in minutes):

Red Line: 5, 12, 7, 15, 11, 12, 6, 10, 9 Blue Line: 9, 9, 26, 6, 10, 8, 11, 10, 8

You should wait in the Blue Line. This is because the Red Line has a median wait time of 10 minutes while the Blue Line has a median wait time of 9 minutes. This is found by first listing the data points in order from least to greatest and finding the middle number, which is the median of the data. Crossing off the numbers on the left and right side until reaching the middle will find the middle number: Red Line: 5, 6, 7, 9, 10, 11, 12, 12, 15 and Blue Line: 6, 8, 8, 9, 9, 10, 10, 11, 26.

Example problem 4

You have gathered data on the wait times for two different lines at the ballpark. You decide to wait in the Blue Line because it has the lower median wait time. Your friend tells you, however, that you should wait in the Red Line because it has the shortest wait time recorded. Consider the data below, decide if you should change your mind and take your friend's advice.

Time (in minutes):
Red Line: 5, 12, 7, 15, 11, 12, 6, 10, 9   Blue Line: 9, 9, 26, 6, 10, 8, 11, 10, 8

You should not take your friend's advice. You should still choose the Blue Line because the Blue Line's median is 9 minutes, while the Red Line's median is 10 minutes. The data point of 26 in the Blue Line is considered an outlier because it varies greatly from the median compared to the other data points in the set. If you ignore that outlier, the median is still 9! Even ignoring the highest wait time for each line, the mean wait time is higher for the red line, so although the Red Line had the shortest wait time and Blue Line had the longest wait time that is not the best judge of predicting wait time.

<u>Example problem 5</u>

Predict what the median of the data is by analyzing the dot plot below.
Calculate the median to check the prediction.

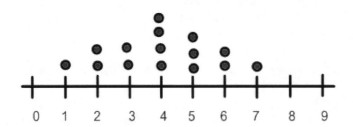

It appears that the median of the data is 4, as its values fall in the middle of all of the dots on the dot plot. Calculating the median is done by first listing the data in order from least to greatest. Each dot on the dot plot represents the number it is above, so therefore the data values are
$1, 2, 2, 3, 3, 4, 4, 4, 4, 5, 5, 5, 6, 6, 7$. To find the median the values must be crossed off until the middle number is reached:
$1, 2, 2, 3, 3, 4, 4, 4, 4, 5, 5, 5, 6, 6, 7$. The appearance of the median in the dot plot is accurate, as the median is 4.

Statistical questions and variability

Determine whether the following questions are considered statistical questions and explain why or why not:
'How many pets do the families in my neighborhood have?'
'What size are my shoes?'
'How many pages did I read in the last hour?'
'How long did it take the students in my class to get to school today?'

Yes, this is a statistical question because it will have variability. The families in your neighborhood will not each have the same number of pets, but there will be a variation in the data collected and conclusions can be drawn from this.

No, this is not a statistical question. There will be no variation because there is one answer.

No, this is not a statistical question. There will be no variation because there is one answer.

Yes, this is a statistical question because it has variability. There will be many different answers to this question and conclusions can be drawn from the data.

Data representation and analysis

Example problem 1

Represent the following data in a dot plot and find the mode of the data:
The amount of money your friends make babysitting per hour
5, 2, 7, 9, 4, 5, 6, 7, 9, 7
The data is represented in a dot plot below:

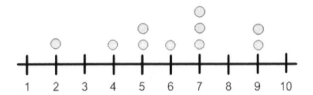

The amount of money your friends make babysitting per hour

This is made by creating a number line that can display the range of data and then placing one dot above each number for each data value equal to that number. The mode of this data is 7, which is the number that occurs in the data most. The mode is easy to see in a dot plot because it is the number that has the most dots. In this data, three people get $7/hour babysitting while only one or two people get paid the other amounts in the list.

Example problem 2

Represent the following data in a box plot:
Michael's math test grades last semester
88, 90, 95, 82, 98, 90, 77, 89, 91

The data is represented in the box plot below:

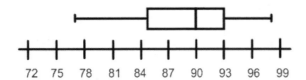

Michael's math test grades last semester

This is made by creating a number line that will fit the distribution of the data and then determining the five points that are needed to create the box plot, which are: the minimum, the maximum, the median, the lower quartile, and the upper quartile. The minimum is the number in the list with the least value, 77, and the maximum is the number with the greatest value, 98. A small tick mark is placed above those two values on the number line. The median of the data is 90, which is found by listing the data in order from least to greatest and finding the number in the middle: 77, 82, 88, 89, 90, 90, 91, 95, 98. The lower quartile is the median of the lower half of the data, which is 85 because the middle of the lower half of the data is between the two middle numbers 82 and 88, and is therefore found by finding their average: $\frac{82+88}{2} = 85$. The upper quartile is the median of the upper half of the data, which is 93 because it is between 91 and 95, and their average is $\frac{91+95}{2} = 93$. A tick mark is placed above the median and upper and lower quartile values on the number line and a box is created around those three marks. A line is then extended from the ends of the box to the minimum and maximum.

<u>Example problem 3</u>

Represent the data below in a histogram:
The amount of homework your friends did last night, in minutes
45, 25, 33, 65, 37, 55, 45, 42, 31, 49, 48, 22

The histogram below represents the data:

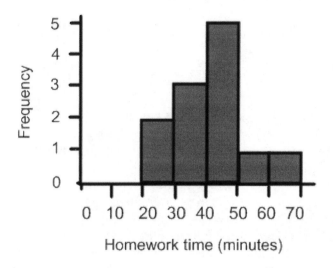

This is made by creating a graph and labeling the x-axis with homework time, the y-axis with frequency, and creating appropriate intervals for each. (Generally, divide the range of the data into 5 – 7 intervals.) The data values in each interval, which are 10 minute intervals in this histogram, are counted to determine the frequency of data values in those intervals. Adjacent rectangles are created to show the distribution of data. There are 2 pieces of data that fall between 20 and 30 minutes, so that interval has a frequency of 2. There are 3 pieces of data that fall between 30 and 40 minutes, so that interval has a frequency of 3. There are 5 pieces of data that fall between 40 and 50 minutes, so that interval has a frequency of 5. And there is 1 piece of data each that falls between 50 and 60 minutes and 60 and 70 minutes, so those each have a frequency of one.

Mr. Smith was deciding which of two intersections to post signs at for his garage sale. He sat at one intersection each day for 30 minute time intervals for two consecutive days. Summarize the meaning of his data recorded below and predict what conclusions he may draw.

Number of cars that drove by

Time	Intersection 1	Intersection 2
7am-7:30	8	1
9am-9:30	10	6
11am-11:30	11	10
1pm-1:30	0	9
3pm-3:30	5	10
5pm-5:30	2	4

Mr. Smith will most likely want to place signs for his garage sale at Intersection 2. This is because over the course of the day that Mr. Smith observed Intersection 2, 40 cars drove by, whereas over the course of the day that he observed Intersection 1, only 36 cars drove by. However, Mr. Smith's data shows observations that might make him choose Intersection 1. For example, Mr. Smith might know that morning hours are usually the busiest for garage sales and thus he might want to put his signs at Intersection 1 because more cars drive through that intersection in the morning hours. But, it seems as though the traffic at Intersection 1 tapers off greatly in the afternoon and Mr. Smith might be more concerned with having the possibility of a steady flow of customers at his garage sale all day.

Example problem 5

The local hospital recorded the lengths of the babies born yesterday, given below. Analyze the data and determine what units were being used in the measurements. With the conclusion justify any changes you would recommend for the collection of the data.
Lengths of Babies
1.5, 1.75, 2, 16, 17.5, 17.5, 18.5, 19, 20, 20, 21, 22

It is clear that there are two different units of measurement being used to measure the lengths of babies. All of the data points between 16 and 22 are reasonable if measured in inches. The data points of 1.5, 1.75, and 2 cannot have been measured in inches and were most likely measured in feet. The data points of 1.5, 1.75, and 2 are reasonable if measured in feet, however all the other pieces of data are not reasonable to have been measured in feet. Therefore, the hospital will need to choose one unit of measure when collecting the data on the lengths of the babies born there. One suggestion would be to measure all babies in inches, and thus change the values of 1.5, 1,75, and 2 in the data to 18, 21, and 24.

Range

The range helps to quantify the amount of variation in a set of data. It is the difference between the maximum value and the minimum value and can be found by subtracting the minimum value in a set from the maximum value in a set.

Example problem 1

> *Find the range of each situation below and describe its meaning:*
> *The height of students in Mickey's class (in inches):*
> *58, 62, 59, 61.5, 61, 58, 60, 59.5, 61, 58, 59, 61, 60.5, 58.5*
> *The amount of money each friend spent at dinner (in dollars):*
> *15, 7, 11.50, 21, 14, 17.50, 10, 9, 23.50, 14*
>
> For the height of students in Mickey's class the range is 4 inches. The maximum height is 62 inches and the minimum height is 58 inches, so therefore the range is $62 - 58 = 4$. This means that all students in Mickey's class are fairly close together in height as this is a small range to hold all of the data. If the whole class was lined up the difference in height from the tallest person to the shortest would be only 4 inches.
> For the amount of money each friend spent at dinner, the range is $16.50. The maximum value is $23.50 and the minimum value is $7, so therefore the range is $23.50 - 7 = 16.50$. This means that the friends spent a wide range at dinner, meaning some friends bought much more expensive meals or more food than some of the others.

Example problem 2

> *The following data shows the cost of used cars in the sales lot. Plot the data on a line plot and describe the meaning of the range of data.*
> *Price of Used Cars For Sale (in dollars)*

14,000	7,500	8,000	600
19,000	18,500	9,500	3,000
5,500		950	16,000 2,000

> *The data is displayed on the line plot below:*

Price of cars (in dollars)

The range of the data is $18,400. This is found by subtracting the smallest value, $600, from the largest value, $19,000. This is a large range for the price of the cars in the lot. Looking at the line plot it is easy to see that the prices of cars are very spread out. This might mean that the lot has some fairly new used cars and also some very old cars for sale.

<u>Example problem 3</u>

The following table shows the amount of television each student watched the night before the math test. Any student who watched television for a greater amount of time than the median earned a D on the test. Find the range of the data and determine who got a D on the test.

Student	Hours of TV watched	Student	Hours of TV watched
Billy	1	Brock	2
Paige	6	Colleen	3.5
Margaret	.5	Courtney	0
Skylar	2	Blair	3
James	0	Theresa	1
Fiona	0	Tyler	4.5
Kyle	3	Troy	1.5

The range of the data is 6 hours. This is found by subtracting the smallest value, 0, from the largest value, 6.

The median of the data must be found in order to determine who earned a D on the test. The median of the data is 1.75 hours. This is found by ordering the numbers from least to greatest and finding the middle number, like so: $0, 0, 0, .5, 1, 1, 1.5, 2, 2, 3, 3, 3.5, 4.5, 6$. Since there are two numbers in the middle of the data, the average of those two must be found. Therefore, the median of the data is $\frac{1.5+2}{2} = \frac{3.5}{2} = 1.75$. Since any student who watched TV for more than 1.75 hours earned a D on the test, Paige, Skylar, Kyle, Brock, Colleen, Blair, and Tyler all earned D's on the test.

<u>Example problem 4</u>

The students in Mark's class filled in the table to represent how many siblings they each have. Use the table to find the range of the data and describe the shape made by a line plot of the data.

Number of siblings	Number of students
0	||
1	||||
2	⊬⊦⊦||
3	|||
4	||
5	
6	|

The range of the data is 6. This is found by subtracting the smallest number, 0, from the largest number, 6. The shape of the line plot of this data is similar to a bell curve, or that of a small hill. The majority of the dots are above the 2, which is the mode of the data because it occurs most frequently. It is also the median of the data, because it is the value in the middle. The dots on either side of 2 are similar-sized groups getting smaller the farther away from 2 the values get. This can be seen in the line plot below:

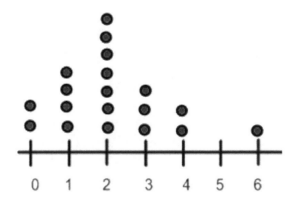

<u>Example problem 5</u>

Given the following graph of data of four students' speeds to walk to school, determine what units must have been used.

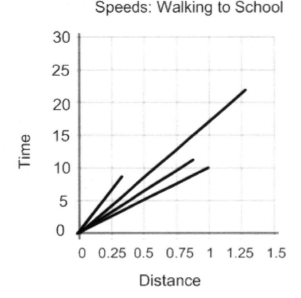

Speeds: Walking to School

The units that must have been used are Distance in Miles and Time in Minutes. If the distance measurement is considered first, there is no other reasonable measurement other than miles. It would not make sense for the measurements to be in feet, as walking less than 1.5 feet to school would not be considered because everyone has to walk at least a few feet to get into the building, and no one can live 1.5 feet from the school. Similarly, meters or yards or anything less than those would also not be a reasonable measurement.

Considering that the distance is measured in miles, the most likely unit of time measurement is in minutes. Hours is very unreasonable as it would not take someone over 20 hours to walk 1.25 miles, and seconds is as equally unreasonable as it would not take someone just over 20 seconds to walk 1.25 miles.

The only other possible measurement would be distance in kilometers, but the times in minutes are maybe a little too slow to represent walking distances in kilometers.

Important terms

Sample size - Sample size is the number of people surveyed or the number of observations made in a statistical experiment. For example, if the mayor of a town surveyed 800 residents to determine the town's opinion on a new park, then the sample size is 800 and the mayor has hopefully judged that this will be a large enough sample to represent the whole population.

- 48 -

Data set - Data set is a list, or set, of all the numbers or values that are the results from a statistical experiment. An example would be that the following data set represents the shoe sizes of Fred's friends: {6, 7.5, 8, 8, 8.5, 9.5, 10}. That list of numbers is the data set and each number represents the shoe size of Fred's friends.

First quartile - The first quartile is the number that is the median of the lower half of a data set that is, the half between the minimum and the median. All pieces of data less than the first quartile are in the lowest 25% of the data. It can also be referred to as the 'lower quartile'.

Second quartile - The second quartile is more commonly called the median, and is the middle number of a data set. It splits the data in half, so that 50% of the data is less than this number and 50% of the data is greater than this number.

Third quartile - The third quartile is the number that is the median of the upper half of a data set, that is, the half between the median and the maximum. All pieces of data greater than it are in the top 25% of the data. It can also be referred to as the 'upper quartile'.

Maximum - The maximum is the greatest value in a data set.

Minimum - The minimum is the least value in a data set.

Expressions and Equations

Variables, numbers, and operation symbols

<u>Examples</u>

Use variables, numbers, and operation symbols to express the following:
*3 less than a number **n***
*The quotient of 4 and a number **x***
*The difference between 10 and **y***
*The product of 12 and **m***
*The sum of **x** and 4*
*6 more than a number **r***

"3 less than a number n" means taking 3 away from the value of n, so this is expressed as $n - 3$.

"The quotient of 4 and a number x" means dividing 4 by x, so we write $\frac{4}{x}$.

"The difference between 10 and y" means subtracting y from 10, so we write $10 - y$.

"The product of 12 and m" means multiplying 12 and m, so we write $12 \times m$, or simply $12m$.

"The sum of x and 4" means adding x and 4, so we write $x +\_4$.

"6 more than a number r" means adding 6 to r, so we write $r +6$.

Properties

Example problem 1

State which property is being used in each number sentence:

$$2x + y = y + 2x$$
$$5 \times (x + 1) = (5 \times x) + (5 \times 1)$$
$$3 \times 1 = 3$$
$$6 \times m \times n = m \times n \times 6$$
$$4 \times (5a) = (4a) \times 5$$
$$s + 0 = s$$
$$10 + (6 + 1) = (10 + 6) + 1$$

The Commutative Property of Addition is shown here, which states that you can add terms in any order.

The Distributive Property is shown here, which states that a number multiplied to an expression in parentheses must be multiplied to every term in the parentheses.

The Identity Property of Multiplication is shown here, which states that multiplying a number or term by 1 does not change its value.

The Commutative Property of Multiplication is shown here, which states that you can multiply terms in any order.

The Associative Property of Multiplication is shown here, which states that any group of numbers and/or variables can be grouped together in parentheses to be multiplied first before multiplying by the remaining numbers and/or variables.

"$s + 0 = s$" – The Identity Property of Addition is shown here, which states that adding 0 to any number or term does not change the value of that number or term.

The Associative Property of Addition is shown here, which states that any group of numbers and/or variables can be grouped together in parentheses to be added first before adding the remaining numbers and/or variables.

<u>Example problem 2</u>

Simplify the following expressions and state what property, or properties, you used:

A. $3(2x - 1)$
B. $4x + y + 2x - 3y$
C. $2(5 + m) - 2m$
D. $7(2x)$

A. This simplifies to "$6x - 3$". The multiplication by 3 has to be distributed to both terms in the parentheses, which is the Distributive Property.
B. This simplifies to "$6x - 2y$", since combining like terms by adding them first ($4x + 2x = 6x$) and then adding those sums uses the Commutative Property of Addition.
C. This simplifies to 10. This is done using the Distributive Property to first multiply the 2 to each term in the parentheses to get "$10 + 2m - 2m$" and then combining like terms, using the Commutative Property of Addition. Since the like terms in this case are a positive $2m$ and a negative $2m$, they add to zero and therefore the answer is simply 10.
D. This simplifies to "$14x$" using the Associative Property of Multiplication.

<u>Example problem 3</u>

Use the distributive property to match one expression in Column I with an equivalent expression in Column II.

Column I	Column II
A. 4(3x-1)	U. 10x+25y
B. 8(9+2x)	V. 12x-4
C. 36-2x	W. 3(4x-8y)
D. 4(4a+5)	X. 72+16x
E. 12x-24y	Y. 2(18-x)
F. 5(2x+5y)	Z. 16a+20

A is equivalent to V, by distributing the '4' into the parentheses.
B is equivalent to X by distributing the '8' into the parentheses.
C is equivalent to Y by distributing the '2' in Y back into the parentheses, or by factoring 2 from both the '36' and the '$2x$'.
D is equivalent to Z by distributing the '4' into the parentheses.
E is equivalent to W by distributing the '3' in W back into the parentheses, or by factoring '3' from both the '$12x$' and '$24y$'.
F is equivalent to U by distributing the '5' into the parentheses.

Expressions

<u>Example problem 1</u>

Simplify the following expressions:

$$(x + 2) \times (x + 2) \times (x + 2)$$
$$(3 - y) \times (3 - y) \times (4x) \times (4x) \times (4x)$$
$$(5 - m) \times (5 - m)^2 \times (6 - m)$$

$(x + 2) \times (x + 2) \times (x + 2) = (x + 2)^3$ This is because there are three instances of $(x + 2)$ being multiplied together, which is the same as raising the quantity $(x + 2)$ to the third power.

$(3 - y) \times (3 - y) \times (4x) \times (4x) \times (4x) = (3 - y)^2 \times (4x)^3$ This is because there are two instances of $(3 - y)$ being multiplied together, which is the same as raising the entity $(3 - y)$ to the second power. That is then being multiplied by three instances of $(4x)$, which is the same as multiplying by $(4x)$ raised to the third power.

$(5 - m) \times (5 - m)^2 \times (6 - m) = (5 - m)^3 \times (6 - m)$ This is because there are three instances of $(5 - m)$ being multiplied together, because $(5 - m)^2 = (5 - m) \times (5 - m)$.

<u>Example problem 2</u>

Evaluate the following:

$$(3 - 1) + 4^2 \times 2$$
$$3^3 + (3 \times 3)$$
$$5^2 - (6 - 2)^2$$

Evaluate these expressions following the order of operations: parentheses, exponents, multiplication/division, and addition/subtraction.

$(3 - 1) + 4^2 \times 2$ is equivalent to 34: $(3 - 1) + 4^2 \times 2 = (2) + 4^2 \times 2 = (2) + 16 \times 2 = (2) + 32 = 34$
$3^3 + (3 \times 3)$ is equivalent to 36: $3^3 + (3 \times 3) = 3^3 + 9 = 27 + 9 = 36$
$5^2 - (6 - 2)^2$ is equivalent to 9: $5^2 - (6 - 2)^2 = 5^2 - (4)^2 = 25 - 16 = 9$

Example problem 3

Simplify the following expressions and identify the terms, products, factors, sums, quotients, and/or coefficients in each:

A. $4x + 3x - 2y$
B. $10(3 + 1)$
C. $\dfrac{10+5+1}{2}$

There are three terms in the original expression, $4x, 3x,$ and $-2y$. There are also three coefficients in the expression, $4, 3,$ and -2, respectively. Since $7x$ is the sum of $4x$ and $3x$, the expression simplifies to $7x - 2y$.

There are two terms in the original expression, 3 and 1, and one coefficient, 10, multiplying the sum of the two terms. The sum of 3 and 1 is 4, and the product of 10 and 4 is 40. Therefore, 10 and 4 are factors of 40.

Since we can write this as $(10 + 5 + 1) \div 2$, there are four terms in the original expression, $10, 5, 1$ and 2. The sum of $10, 5,$ and 1 is 16, and the quotient of 16 and 2 is 8. Therefore, 2 and 8 are factors of 16.

Example problem 4

Write expressions to represent the following situations:
Turner has saved \$75 toward the purchase of an iPod. How much more money does he need to save?
This week Marcus mowed twice the amount of lawns he mowed last week. How many lawns did Marcus mow this week?
Jenny earns \$4 for every room she cleans in her house. How much money will she earn cleaning her whole house?

Turner has saved \$75 toward the purchase of an iPod. The amount of money he still needs to save can be expressed by $C - 75$, representing the difference between total cost, C, of the iPod and what he already has.

This week Marcus mowed twice the amount of lawns he mowed last week. The number of lawns he mowed this week can be expressed as $2l$, representing two times the number of lawns mowed last week, l.

Jenny earns \$4 for every room she cleans in her house. The amount of money she will earn cleaning her whole house can be expressed by $4r$, representing 4 times the number of rooms, r, in her whole house.

Example problem 5

Write expressions to represent the following situations and then solve them:
Caroline has 3 more hours of homework tonight than last night. How much
homework does Caroline have tonight if she had one hour of homework last
night?
This month Fred will only work one-third of the hours he worked last month.
How many hours will Fred work this month if he worked 150 hours last
month?

The first part of this situation can be expressed by $h + 3$, representing the number of hours of homework Caroline has tonight in terms of 3 more than she had last night, h. If she had one hour of homework last night, then she has 4 hours of homework tonight, because $1 + 3 = 4$.

This can be expressed by $\frac{w}{3}$, representing the number of hours Fred will work this month in terms of one third of the number he worked last month, w. If he worked 150 hours last month, then he will work 50 hours this month, because $\frac{150}{3} = 50$.

Writing equations

Example problem 1

Write and solve equations that represent the following situations:
You are 16 years old and twice as old as your sister. How old is your sister?
Your mother is 5 times as old as your sister. How old is your mother?
Your cousin's age is the sum of your age and your sister's age. How old is your
cousin?

This situation is represented by the equation $2x = 16$, where x represents your sister's age. Solve this equation by dividing both sides by 2, resulting in $x = 8$. Therefore, your sister is 8 years old.

Before we knew your sister's age, this was represented by $m = 5x$, where m is your mother's age and x is your sister's. Since it is now known that your sister is 8 years old, this situation is represented by the equation $5 \times 8 = m$. Solving this equation gives an answer of $5 \times 8 = 40$, so your mother is 40 years old.

Until we knew your sister's age, this was represented by $c = 16 + x$. Since your sister is 8 years, this situation can be represented by the equation $16 + 8 = c$, where c represents your cousin's age. Solving this equation gives an answer of $16 + 8 = 24$, so your cousin is 24 years old.

Example problem 2

Determine the equation that represents the cost, C, for any number of shirts, x, using the table of information below, and find how much it will cost to buy 12 shirts:

Number of Shirts	Cost (in dollars)
1	5
2	10
3	15
4	20

The equation that represents the situation is $C = 5x$. This is found by determining the relationship between the independent variable, which is the number of t-shirts, and the dependent variable, which is the cost. In the table it can be seen that for each shirt bought, the cost goes up by 5 dollars. It is then also seen that multiplying the number of shirts by 5 gives the cost, because $1 \times 5 = 5, 2 \times 5 = 10, 3 \times 5 = 15,$ and $4 \times 5 = 20$. Therefore, for any x number of shirts, that number can just be multiplied by 5 to get the cost, which is represented by $C = 5x$.

It will cost $60 to buy 12 shirts. This is found by using the equation that represents the data, substituting 12 for x, the number of shirts: $C = 5 \times 12 = 60$.

Example problem 3

Write the equation to represent the following table of values and graph them.
Using the graph, predict the cost of mailing a 6 pound package.

The cost of mailing a package at the post office.	
Weight (in lbs)	Cost (in dollars)
1	1.5
2	3
3	4.5
4	6

The equation that represents the cost, C, in terms of the weight, w, of a package is $C = 1.5w$, because for each additional pound, the cost increases by $1.50 per pound. These values are graphed in the graph below:

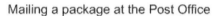

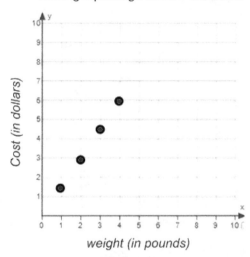

Mailing a package at the Post Office

Looking at the graph, the points are going up at a constant rate of $1.50 for each pound. The next point would be at (5, 7.5), and then the next point would be at (6, 9). This means that the cost of mailing a 6 pound package would be $9.

Checking equations

Example problem 1

> *Match each expression in Column I with its equivalent expression in Column II. Verify that the expressions are equivalent by substituting any non-zero value for x.*

Column I
A. $4x$
B. $10x + 12$
C. x

Column II
X. $x + 2x + x$
Y. $3x - x - x$
Z. $3x + 5 + 7x + 7$

A is equivalent to X. If $x = 3$, we see that $4x = 4 \times 3 = 12$, and $x + 2x + x = 3 + 2 \times 3 + 3 = 3 + 6 + 3 = 12$. Since the expressions have the same value when $x = 3$, the expressions are equivalent.

B is equivalent to Z. If $x = 2$, we see that B $= 10x + 12 = 10 \times 2 + 12 = 20 + 12 = 32$, and Z $= 3x + 5 + 7x + 7 = 3 \times 2 + 5 + 7 \times 2 + 7 = 6 + 5 + 14 + 7 = 32$. Since the expressions have the same value when $x = 2$, the expressions are equivalent.

C is equivalent to Y. If $x = 5$, we see that $x = 5$, and $3x - x - x = 3 \times 5 - 5 - 5 = 15 - 5 - 5 = 10 - 5 = 5$. Since the expressions have the same value when $x = 5$, the expressions are equivalent.

Example problem 2

> *The equation $y = 2x + 5$ represents the line that contains all points (x, y) that satisfy the equation. Decide which, if any, of the following points lie on the line.*
> $$(1,8) \qquad (0,5) \qquad (2,9) \qquad (2,5)$$

The points $(0,5)$ *and* $(2,9)$ lie on the line. Any points that lie on the line have x and y values that make the equation true. Plug in the first value of each pair for x and the second value of each pair for y, and see whether the equation is true. For the point $(0,5)$: $5 = 2 \times 0 + 5 = 0 + 5 = 5$, and the equation is still true. For the point $(2,9)$: $9 = 2 \times 2 + 5 = 4 + 5 = 9$, and the equation is still true. These points make the equation true and lie on the line. The other two points do not work in the equation. For $(1,8)$: $8 = 2 \times 1 + 5 = 2 + 5 \neq 7$. For $(2,5)$: $5 = 2 \times 2 + 5 = 4 + 5 \neq 9$. (This could also be discovered by referring back to the point $(2,9)$ that is on the line. Since y equals 9 when x is 2, the point $(2,5)$ could be eliminated without testing it in the equation.)

<u>Example problem 3</u>

Solve the inequality for a and check the answer by plugging in a possible value:
$$2a + 6 > 30$$

The solution is $a > 12$. This means that a can be any value greater than 12. This is solved the same way an equation is solved, doing whatever is done to one side of the inequality to the other:

$2a + 6 > 30$ (first subtract 6 from both sides)
$2a > 24$ (divide both sides by 2)
$a > 12$

To check the solution, any value that is greater than 12 can be chosen for a. If 20 is chosen, check to see that the left side of the inequality will have a greater value than 30:

$2 \times 20 + 6 > 30$
$40 + 6 > 30$
$46 > 30$

Because it is true that 46 is greater than 30, the inequality was solved correctly.

<u>Example problem 4</u>

Find the solution to the following equation and check the solution by plugging it back into the equation:
$$2p - 11 = 19$$

The solution is $p = 15$. This is found by manipulating the equation to get p by itself on one side of the equal sign. This can be done best by getting rid of the numbers in the reverse order of the normal order of operations. Surrounding the p there is a 2 being multiplied to it and an 11 being subtracted from it. In order of operations, multiplication would be done first and subtraction after, so to undo this expression the subtraction must be handled first, then the multiplication:

$2p - 11 = 19$ (first add 11 to both sides to undo the subtraction by 11)
$2p = 30$ (then divide both sides by 2 to undo the multiplication by 2)
$p = 15$

By plugging the solution back into the original equation it can be verified: $2 \times 15 - 11 = 30 - 11 = 19 = 19$. Since both sides of the equation have a value of 19, the solution is correct.

Table representing an equation

<u>Example</u>

The equation $T = 1l$, represents T, the total time in minutes a racecar driver drives for l number of laps. Determine what the 1 in the equation means, and make a table of values that represents this equation and graph them.

The 1 in the equation represents the time the driver takes to complete one lap. This means that every lap takes the driver 1 minute. The table and graph below show this data:

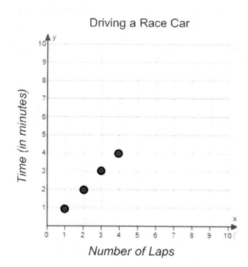

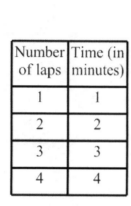

Number of laps	Time (in minutes)
1	1
2	2
3	3
4	4

- 60 -

Inequalities

Example problem 1

> Write inequalities to represent the following situations, and graph them on number lines:
> The speed limit on the highway is 65mph.
> Your teacher is older than 30 years old.

A. This is represented by the inequality $x \leq 65$, because a person can drive at any speed less than or equal to 65mph. This is graphed on the number line below, showing a closed circle on the 65 and an arrow shading to the left, because the safe speeds include 65 and anything less than it:

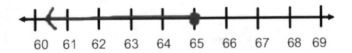

B. This is represented by the inequality $x > 30$, because your teacher is any age greater than 30 years old, but not equal to 30. This is graphed on the number line below, showing an open circle at 30 and an arrow shading to the right, which means that 30 is not included in the possible ages for your teacher but any number greater is:

Example problem 2

> Write inequalities to represent the following situations, and give one possible solution for each:
> You will not go to school for more than 5 days this week.
> Your dad makes at least $100 a day at work.
> The bowling alley requires a birthday party size of less than 20 kids.

This is represented by the inequality $x \leq 5$, because you might go to school 5 days or you might go to school any amount less than that. One solution could be 4, because you might get sick one day this week and only go to school 4 days.

This is represented by the inequality $x \geq 100$, because your dad will make $100 or more at work each day. One solution could be $125.

This is represented by the inequality $x < 20$, because there cannot be 20 kids in the party but there can be any amount less than that. One solution could be 15 kids at the birthday party.

Example problem 3

Write inequalities to represent the following situations, and graph them on number lines:
The minimum cost of a school photo package is $10.
A person has to be less than 48 inches tall to ride the kiddie rides at the amusement park.

This statement is represented by the inequality $x \geq 10$, because you can spend $10 or more on photos. This is graphed on the number line below, showing a closed circle on the 10 and an arrow shading to the right, because the amount you can spend includes 10 dollars or any number greater than that.

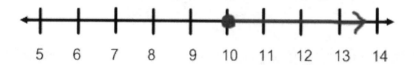

This statement is represented by the inequality $x < 48$ because the acceptable heights are all those less than 48 inches. This is graphed on the number line below, showing an open circle on the 48 and an arrow shading to the left, because 48 is not included in the acceptable heights, but anything less than it is:

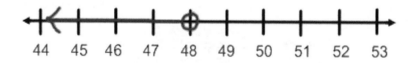

Independent variable and dependent variable

The independent variable is that quantity in a situation that affects the value of the other when changed.

The dependent variable is that quantity in a situation that depends on the value of another variable.

For the following examples:
The total amount of money m you earn for mowing n lawns.
The price p you pay for renting x videos.
The distance d you travel on a bus over time t.

The number of lawns you mow, n, is the independent variable, while the amount of money you earn, m, will depend on how many lawns you mow and thus is the dependent variable.

The number of videos, x, you rent is the independent variable, and the price, p, you pay is the dependent variable because it depends on how many videos you rent.

The time, t, is the independent variable, and the distance, d, is the dependent variable because the distance you travel will depend on how long you travel for.

Important terms

Quotient - The result of a division operation. For example, the quotient of 10 and 5 is 2.

Product - The result of a multiplication operation. For example, the product of 6 and 3 is 18.

Sum - The result of an addition operation. For example, the sum of 4 and 7 is 11.

Difference - The result of a subtraction operation. The difference between two numbers can be thought of as the distance between them on a number line. For example, the difference of 12 and 8 is 4.

Factor - A factor is a number divides evenly into a given number. For example, 4 is a factor of 8, because 8 is evenly divisible by 4.

Coefficient - A coefficient is a number that multiplies a variable and that denotes how many instances of that variable are represented together. This number is written in front of, or to the left of, the variable. There is generally no multiplication sign between the coefficient and the variable. For example, in the term '3x', 3 is the coefficient.

Term - A term is a number or variable or a product of number(s) and/or variable(s) that does not contain an operation symbol. For example, in the expression $y + 4x + 7$, y, 4x, and 7 are separate terms.

Expression - An expression is a group of one or more numbers variables, and/or terms that are combined together with operations. There is no equal sign in an expression. For example, $7x - (2x + 3) \div 4$ is an expression.

Variable - A variable is an unknown value represented by a letter in an expression or equation. A variable can represent one value or a set of values. For example, in the equation $2x + 4 = 10$, x is a variable and has one value. In the equation $y = 8x + 1$, x and y can have multiple values as long as they both make the equation true.

Equation - An equation is a relationship equating two expressions. An equation can be distinguished from an expression by the equal sign. For example, $4x = 12$ is an equation because it has an equal sign.

Inequality - An inequality is a comparison between two or more expressions that are not necessarily equal; one might be greater or less than another. Because of this, when solving an inequality for a variable, the solution is a range of values. For example, $5a + 2 \le 22$ is an inequality because it has a "less than or equal to" symbol between the two expressions.

Practice Test #1

Practice Questions

1. Antonio wants to buy a roll of border to finish an art project. At four different shops, he found four different borders he liked. He wants to use the widest of the borders. The list shows the width, in inches, of the borders he found.

$$1\frac{7}{10} , 1.72 , 1\frac{3}{4} , 1.695$$

Which roll of border should Antonio buy if he wants to buy the widest border?

Ⓐ $1\frac{7}{10}$

Ⓑ 1.72

Ⓒ $1\frac{3}{4}$

Ⓓ 1.695

2. Daniella wrote a decimal and a fraction which were equivalent to each other. Which pair of numbers could be the pair Daniella wrote?

Ⓐ $0.625, \frac{7}{8}$

Ⓑ $0.375, \frac{3}{8}$

Ⓒ $0.75, \frac{7}{5}$

Ⓓ $0.45, \frac{4}{5}$

3. Glenda poured salt into three salt shakers from a box that contained 19 ounces of salt. She poured 5 ounces of salt into one shaker. She divided what was left evenly into the other two shakers. Which equation best represents this scenario?

Ⓐ 19-5-2(7)=0

Ⓑ 5+2+7=19

Ⓒ 19-2-7-7=0

Ⓓ 19-2(5)-7=0

4. Large boxes of canned beans hold 24 cans of beans and small boxes hold 12 cans. One afternoon, Gerald brought 4 large boxes of canned beans and 6 small boxes of canned beans to the food bank. How many cans of beans did Gerald bring to the food bank that afternoon?

Ⓐ 168

Ⓑ 192

Ⓒ 288

Ⓓ 360

5. Enrique used a formula to find the total cost, in dollars, for repairs he and his helper, Jenny, made to a furnace. The expression below shows the formula he used, with 4 being the number of hours he worked on the furnace and 2 being the number of hours Jenny worked on the furnace. $20 + 35(4 + 2) + 47$
What is the total cost for repairing the furnace?

Ⓐ $189

Ⓑ $269

Ⓒ $277

Ⓓ $377

6. One morning at Jim's café, 25 people ordered juice, 10 ordered milk, and 50 ordered coffee with breakfast. Which ratio best compares the number of people who ordered milk to the number of people who ordered juice?

Ⓐ 5 to 7

Ⓑ 5 to 2

Ⓒ 2 to 7

Ⓓ 2 to 5

7. At the middle school Vanessa attends, there are 240 Grade 6 students, 210 Grade 7 students, and 200 Grade 8 students. Which ratio best compares the number of students in Grade 8 to the number of students in Grade 6 at Vanessa's school?

Ⓐ 5 : 6

Ⓑ 5 : 11

Ⓒ 6 : 5

Ⓓ 7 : 8

8. A display at the bottom of the laptop computer Erica was using showed that the battery had a 70% charge. Which decimal is equivalent to 70%?

Ⓐ 0.07

Ⓑ 70.0

Ⓒ 7.0

Ⓓ 0.7

9. The drawing shows a chart used to record completed Math assignments. A checkmark is used to show which assignments are finished.

Math Assignment

✓	✓	✓	✓	✓
✓	✓	✓	✓	✓
✓	✓	✓		
✓	✓			

Which of the following shows the percentage of Math assignments in the chart which are finished?

Ⓐ 15%

Ⓑ 25%

Ⓒ 55%

Ⓓ 75%

10. Harold learned that 6 out of 10 students at his school live within two miles of the school. If 240 students attend Grade 6 at his school, about how many of these students should Harold expect to live within two miles of the school?

Ⓐ 24

Ⓑ 40

Ⓒ 144

Ⓓ 180

11. A unit of liquid measure in the English System of Measure is the gill. The table, shown here, gives conversions from gills to fluid ounces.

Conversion Table

Gills	Fluid Ounces
2	8
4	16
5	20
6	24
10	40

Which equation best describes the relationship between gills, g, and fluid ounces, f?

Ⓐ $f = 8g - 8$

Ⓑ $f = 2g + 4$

Ⓒ $f = 4g$

Ⓓ $4f = g$

12. The table below shows changes in the area of several trapezoids as the lengths of the bases, b_1 and b_2, remain the same and the height, h, changes.

Trapezoids

b_1 (in feet)	b_2 (in feet)	h (in feet)	A (in square feet)
5	7	2	12
5	7	4	24
5	7	6	36
5	7	8	48

Which formula best represents the relationship between A, the areas of these trapezoids, and h, their heights?

Ⓐ $A = 5h$

Ⓑ $A = 6h$

Ⓒ $A = 7h$

Ⓓ $A = 12h$

13. This table shows lengths, widths, and areas of four rectangles. In each rectangle, the length remains 40 meters, but the width changes.

Rectangles

Length	40 meters	40 meters	40 meters	40 meters
Width	20 meters	30 meters	40 meters	50 meters
Perimeter	120 meters	140 meters	160 meters	180 meters

Which formula best represents the relationship between P, the perimeters of these rectangles, and w, their widths?

Ⓐ $P = w + 80$

Ⓑ $P = 2w + 80$

Ⓒ $P = 2(2w + 40)$

Ⓓ $P = 10(w + 40)$

14. Thomas drew a polygon with vertices: A, B, C, and D. He measured the angles formed and recorded the information shown here.

$$m\angle A = 70°, m\angle B = 80°, m\angle C = 120°, m\angle D = 90°$$

Which of the angles that Thomas drew is an obtuse angle?

Ⓐ $\angle A$

Ⓑ $\angle B$

Ⓒ $\angle C$

Ⓓ $\angle D$

15. In $\triangle RST$, shown here, $m\angle S$ is 20° less than $m\angle R$.

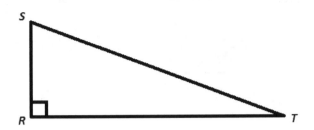

What is the measure of $\angle T$?

Ⓐ 110°

Ⓑ 70°

Ⓒ 50°

Ⓓ 20°

16. Ellen measured $\angle R$ in the parallelogram shown here and found it to be 35°. She knows that $\angle R$ and $\angle T$ have equal measures. She also knows $\angle S$ and $\angle V$ are equal in measure.

What is the measure of $\angle V$?

Ⓐ 215°

Ⓑ 145°

Ⓒ 70°

Ⓓ 35°

17. Which expressions are equivalent to $4(2n-6)$? Select all that apply.

I. $4n(2-6)$
II. $8n-24$
III. $8n+24$
IV. $2(2n-6)+2(2n-6)$
V. $5(2n-6)-(2n-6)$

18. A store buys sodas from the manufacture for $3.60 a case. There are 24 sodas in a case. They sell them for $.35 per soda. How much profit do they make on one soda?

_____

_____

_____

19. Jessica wrote down the times required for five girls to run a race. The times are shown in this list.

25.1 seconds, 24.9 seconds, 25.2 seconds, 24.8 seconds, 25.0 seconds

What time is closest to the total for all five runners?

Ⓐ 1 minute and 5 seconds

Ⓑ 1 minute and 25 seconds

Ⓒ 2 minutes and 5 seconds

Ⓓ 2 minutes and 25 seconds

20. This drawing shows an equilateral triangle and a ruler.

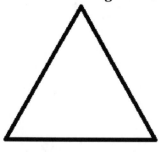

Which is closest to the perimeter of the triangle?

Ⓐ 4.5 centimeters

Ⓑ 9.0 centimeters

Ⓒ 13.5 centimeters

Ⓓ 20.3 centimeters

21. The drawing shows a protractor and a trapezoid.

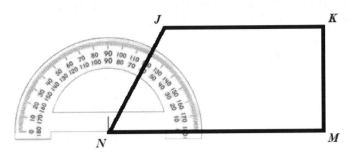

Which is closest to the measure of ∠JNM?

Ⓐ 61°

Ⓑ 79°

Ⓒ 119°

Ⓓ 121°

22. Given the equation $a^2 + (2b - c) \times d$, solve for a=2, b=5, c=8, and d=4. Show your work.

23. Mega Book Store is selling books for 30% off. James wants to buy 3 books. The regular prices of the books are $8, $12, and $15. What is the total price he should expect to pay during the sale?

Ⓐ $35

Ⓑ $25

Ⓒ $24.50

Ⓓ $23.50

24. Stephen researched the topic of solar-powered lights for his science project. He exposed 10 new solar lights to five hours of sunlight. He recorded the number of minutes each light continued to shine after dark in the list below.

63, 67, 73, 75, 80, 91, 63, 72, 79, 87

Which of these numbers is the mean of the number of minutes in Stephen's list?

Ⓐ 28

Ⓑ 63

Ⓒ 74

Ⓓ 75

25. Grade 6 students at Fairview Middle School were asked to name their favorite of six school subjects. The plot below shows a summary of their answers. Each X represents 5 students.

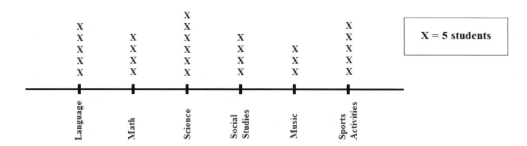

Which graph best represents the data in the plot?

Ⓐ

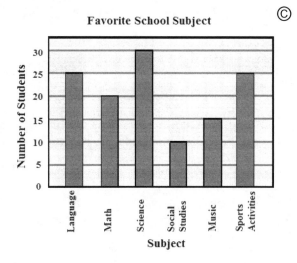

Ⓒ

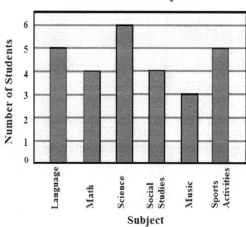

Ⓑ

Ⓓ

- 72 -

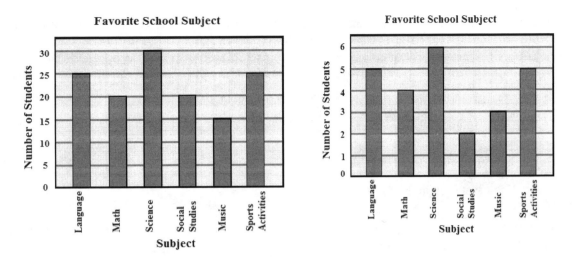

26. Sammie had $120 he had earned doing chores for people in his neighborhood. When school started, he spent $50 for shirts, $30 for jeans, and $40 for school supplies. Which graph best represents how Sammy spent his $120?

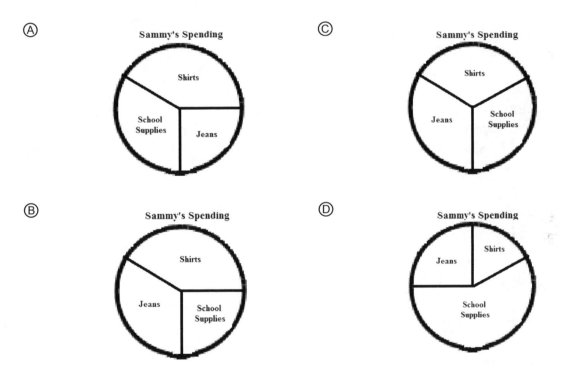

27. James and his driving partner, Larissa, recently drove a truck from Dallas, TX to Los Angeles, CA. The total distance they drove was 1,380 miles. James is paid $0.35 per mile he drives and Larissa is paid $0.30 per mile she drives. What additional information is needed to find the amount James should be paid for the trip?

Ⓐ The total number of hours each person drove

Ⓑ The total number of miles each person drove

Ⓒ The total amount of fuel the truck used

Ⓓ The total weight of the truck and cargo

28. Petra installed 10 light fixtures at a new warehouse that was being built. Each of the fixtures required 3 light bulbs. The bulbs come in packages of 5 and cost $8 per package. What was the total cost for the bulbs required for all of the fixtures Petra installed at the warehouse?

Ⓐ $16

Ⓑ $48

Ⓒ $120

Ⓓ $240

29. Anna and other members of her club sold caps to commemorate their city's 100th birthday. The caps sold for $14 and came in four colors. The club made $3,360 in total sales from selling the caps. The graph below shows the part of the total sales that each color represented.

Colors of Caps Sold

White · Black · Pink · Gray

Which number is closest to the combined number of white and pink caps sold by Anna's club members?

Ⓐ 40

Ⓑ 80

Ⓒ 120

Ⓓ 160

30. Gabe has 6 pencils. The lengths of his pencils in inches are shown on the number line below. What is the mean length of the pencils?

Ⓐ 7 in.

Ⓑ $7\frac{1}{4}$ in.

Ⓒ $7\frac{1}{2}$ in.

Ⓓ $6\frac{3}{4}$ in.

31. Jason wants to put dry fertilizer on the grass in his front yard. The yard is 20 feet wide and 45 feet long. Each pound of the fertilizer he plans to use is enough for 150 square feet. Which procedure could Jason use to determine the correct amount of fertilizer to use on the entire yard?

Ⓐ Divide 150 by 20 and divide 150 by 45, and then add those quotients together

Ⓑ Add 20 and 45, double that total, and then divide that total by 150

Ⓒ Multiply 20 by 45, and then subtract 150 from that product

Ⓓ Multiply 20 by 45, and then divide that product by 150

32. An electronics store sells laptops for $475. They are on sale for $380. Which equation below represents this? Let *r* represent the regular price of laptops and *s* represent the sale price.

Ⓐ $r=.8s$

Ⓑ $s=.2r$

Ⓒ $s=.7r$

Ⓓ $s=.8r$

33. Kerianne collected the weights of her friends. What is the range of her friends' weight?

55 lbs, 63 lbs, 48 lbs, 72 lbs, 61 lbs, 68 lbs

34. What is the greatest common factor of 66 and 24?

_____

_____

_____

35. Point *A* on the graph below is reflected across the x-axis and then translated 3 units left. At what coordinates does it end up?

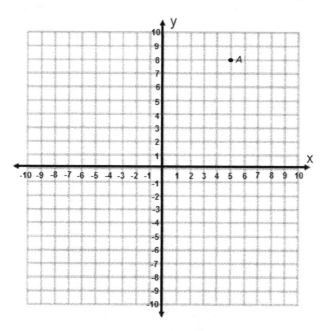

(A) $(2,8)$

(B) $(2,-8)$

(C) $(-2,8)$

(D) $(5,-8)$

36. Candace's shoelace broke. She measured the unbroken shoelace and finds that she needs a replacement lace that is at least 16 inches long. The store has the following lengths available. $15\frac{7}{10}, 16.25, \frac{47}{3}, 15.5$
Which one of the following lace lengths would be long enough to replace the broken shoelace?

(A) $15\frac{7}{10}$

(B) 16.25

(C) $\frac{47}{3}$

(D) 15.5

- 76 -

37. Nadia is working summer jobs. She earns $5 for every dog she walks, $2 for bringing back a trashcan, $1 for checking the mail, and $5 for watering the flowers. Nadia walks 3 dogs, brings back 5 trashcans, checks the mail for 10 neighbors, and waters the flowers at 6 houses. Which expression can be used to find out how much money Nadia earned?

    Ⓐ $2(5) +$6(10) + $1

    Ⓑ $10(6) + $1 + $5

    Ⓒ $5(3+6) + $2(5) + $1(10)

    Ⓓ $15 + $10 + $16

38. Only 8% of the dogs were solid white. Which decimal is equivalent to 8%?

    Ⓐ 0.08

    Ⓑ 80.0

    Ⓒ 8.0

    Ⓓ 0.8

39. Use this grid to answer the question.

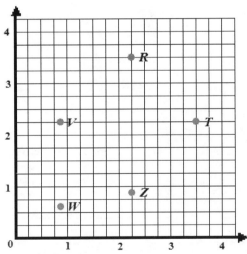

Which of the points on the grid best represents the point at $(2\frac{1}{4}, \frac{7}{8})$?

    Ⓐ T

    Ⓑ V

    Ⓒ W

    Ⓓ Z

40. Part A: A restaurant is trying to attract a younger crowd. They think that they have managed to attract more young people but wanted to graph their results to see. The ages of 40 guests are given below. Create a histogram to show the results.

23	26	21	42	35	29	53	31
19	24	27	30	22	37	21	25
22	26	30	34	27	20	50	41
32	23	18	20	39	22	33	35
25	30	27	19	24	42	47	21

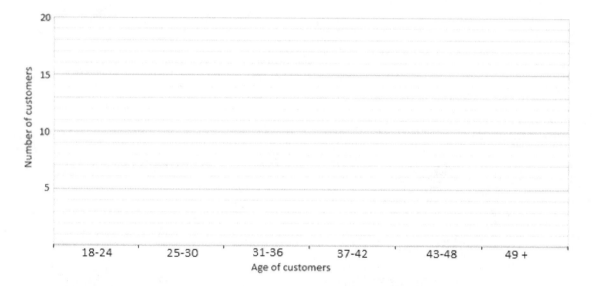

Part B: If they wanted the median age of the customers to be in the 24-30 range were they successful? Explain why or why not.

_____

_____

_____

Answers and Explanations

1. C: To answer this question correctly, convert all numbers to decimal form to make them easy to compare. Since two of the numbers are already in decimal form, we only need to convert $1\frac{7}{10}$ and $1\frac{3}{4}$ to decimal form.

$$7 \div 10 = 0.7, \text{ so } 1\frac{7}{10} = 1.7$$
$$\text{and } 3 \div 4 = 0.75, \text{ so } 1\frac{3}{4} = 1.75$$

Therefore, by comparing place values from left to right of 1.7, 1.72, 1.75 and 1.695, we see that 1.695 is least, 1.7 is next greatest, 1.72 is next, and 1.75 is greatest. So, Antonio should buy the border that is $1\frac{3}{4}$ inches wide.

2. B: To answer this question, one method that can be used is to convert all the fractions to decimal form so it is easier to compare them to each other. This can be done by simply dividing, since the fraction sign means division.

$$7 \div 8 = 0.875$$
$$3 \div 8 = 0.375$$
$$7 \div 5 = 1.4$$
$$4 \div 5 = 0.8$$

So, the only pair of numbers in which the fraction is equivalent to the decimal is in answer B.

3. A: She starts with 19 ounces and then subtracts 5. Then she has 14 ounces and divides that by 2 which gives her 7 ounces per shaker. Thus the equation: 19-5-2(7)=0

4. A: Multiply 24 by 4 to get 96 and multiply 12 by 6 to get 72. Then, add 96 and 72 to get the correct answer, 168.

5. C: To solve this formula, follow the order of operations. First, add what is in the parenthesis, 4 + 2, to get 6. Then, multiply the 6 by 35 to get 210. Last, we should add 20 + 210 + 47 to get 277.

6. D: Note that the ratio asked for is the number of people who ordered milk to the number who ordered juice. The number of people who ordered coffee does not matter here. This compares 10 to 25, and the order is important here. Since the ratio is with the number of people who ordered milk first, the 10 must come first. So, the ratio is 10 to 25, but the ratio can be written in simpler form by dividing both numbers in the ratio by 5, to get the ratio: 2 to 5.

7. A: One way to answer this question is to name the ratio: 200 to 240, then write the ratio in simplest terms by dividing both terms by the greatest common factor, 40, to get 5 to 6. It should be noted that the number of Grade 7 students is not important for this problem. Also, the order of the ratio matters. Since it asks for the ratio using the number of Grade 8 students first, the ratio is 200 to 240 and not the other way around.

8. D: To correctly write a percent as a decimal, the percent sign is dropped and the number is rewritten with the decimal point two places to the left. This is because a percent is always a value out of 100 and the second place after the decimal point is the hundredths place. So, 70% = 0.70 and the zero at the end after the decimal can be dropped.

9. D: There are 15 of the 20 assignments with check marks indicating a finished assignment. Since the fraction $\frac{1}{20}$ represents 5%, then 15 times 5% gives 75% of the assignments finished.

10. C: One way to find this answer is to set up a proportion: $\frac{6}{10} = \frac{G}{240}$, in which G represents the number of Grade 6 students living within two miles of the school. To solve the proportion, we should cross-multiply. So, 10 times G = 6 times 240. This gives the equation: $10G = 1,440$. To solve the equation we divide both sides of the equation by 10, which gives G = 144.

11. C: Looking at the chart, a pattern can be seen in the relationship between the number of gills and the number of fluid ounces. Each number of gills in the first column, when multiplied by 4, gives the number of fluid ounces in the second column. So, f equals 4 times g, or $f = 4g$.

12. B: The formula for the area of trapezoids is not necessarily needed here to do this problem. Since the relationship between the area, A, and the height, h, can be seen in the chart, looking at the third and fourth columns to see if there is a pattern will show a relationship between the variables. Each value in the area column is equal to 6 times the value in the height column. So, we get $A = 6h$.

13. B: To answer this question, start with the perimeter formula, $P = 2(l + w)$ and substitute values that are known to remain the same. So, $P = 2(l + w)$ becomes $P = 2(40 + w)$. Then we distribute, multiplying both numbers inside the parenthesis by 2 and get $P = 80 + 2w$. Writing the variable first in the expression gives us: $P = 2w + 80$.

14. C: An obtuse angle measures between 90 and 180 degrees and $\angle C$ is the only choice which measured in that range.

15. D: The box symbol shown at $\angle R$ means that $\angle R$ measures 90°. Since we are told $m\angle S$ is 20° less than $m\angle R$, subtract 90 –20 to get 70. This means that $m\angle S$ = 70°. The sum of $m\angle R$ and $m\angle S$ is found by adding: 90 +70 = 160. The sum of all angles in a triangle always adds up to 180°, so subtracting 180 – 160 results in a difference of 20. So, $m\angle T$ is 20°.

16. B: The angles opposite each other in a parallelogram are equal in measure. So, $\angle R$ has an equal measure to $\angle T$, or 35°. The sum of the measures of these two angles is 35 + 35 = 70. The sum of the measures of all four angles of a quadrilateral is 360°. We subtract 360 – 70 to get 290. So, 290° is the sum of the measures of the other two equal angles, $\angle S$ and $\angle V$. Then we divide 290 by 2 to get 145. We know that $\angle V$ has a measure of 145°.

17. II, V: First distribute in the 4 to get $8n - 24$. Then do the same for all of the answer choices and see which ones equal $8n - 24$.

18. $.20: First find what it costs the store per coke. So, divide $3.60 by 24 to get $.15 per soda. Then they sell them for $.35 per soda so they make $.20 per soda.

19. C: A close estimate for the total time for all five runners is 125 seconds, which is found by adding 25.1 + 24.9 + 25.2 + 24.8 + 25.0. Then, to convert seconds to minutes, divide by 60 seconds (since there are 60 seconds in a minute) to get 2 with remainder of 5, or 2 minutes and 5 seconds.

20. C: The ruler is used to determine the length of one side of the triangle, which is about 4.5 centimeters. Since this is an equilateral triangle, all three sides are of equal length. To find the perimeter, we add up all of the sides. However, since they are all the same length, we can just multiply 4.5 centimeters by 3 to get 13.5 centimeters.

21. A: Since segment NM lies along the right side of the protractor, we read the inside scale. The segment NM passes between 60° and 70°, much closer to the 60°, so the correct answer is 61°.

22. 12 : First plug all of the numbers into the equation. $2^2 + (2(5) - 8) \times 4$. Then follow the order of operations. $2^2 + 2 \times 4 = 4 + 2 \times 4 = 4 + 8 = 12$.

23. C: First add the costs of all 3 books together to get $35. Then find out what 30% of $35 is. This can be done by multiplying it times .3 to get $10.50. Then subtract $10.50 from $35 and you have the sale price of $24.50.

24. D: The mean is just the average. To calculate this, find the total of all 10 numbers by adding. Then, divide that total by 10 because that is the number of data points. The total is 750, so the mean of this group of numbers is 75

25. B: Notice that the vertical scale should be 0 to 30 by 5's since each of the X's in the plot represent 5 students. Also, each column should represent a number from the line plot. For example, since Language and Sports Activities both show 5 X's, and each X represents 5 students, 5 times 5 = 25. The subjects of Math and Social Studies both show 4 X's, so 4 times 5 = 20. All of the values are found in this way and the only chart that shows these values is B.

26. A: The appropriate fractions can be found by putting the amount of money spent on each category over the total amount of money spent. $\frac{50}{120}$ is a little less than half, since half of 120 is 60. $\frac{30}{120}$ simplifies to $\frac{1}{4}$ and $\frac{40}{120}$ simplifies to $\frac{1}{3}$. This means that Sammy spent almost $\frac{1}{2}$ his money on shirts, $\frac{1}{4}$ of his money on jeans, and $\frac{1}{3}$ of his money on school supplies. The graph in A best represents those fractions.

27. B: Since each person is paid by the number of miles driven, one must know not the total miles for the trip, but the miles each person drove. The fuel, weight, or hours do not matter for this problem.

28. B: To answer this question, find the total number of bulbs required by multiplying 10 by 3. The number of packages of bulbs required can be found by dividing this total number of bulbs, 30, by 5, to find that 6 packages are needed. Then, multiplying 6 by the cost per package, 8, we find that the total cost for all the bulbs needed was $48.

29. D: To answer this question, the total number of caps sold must be found by dividing the total sales, 3,360, by the price of each cap, 14. 3,360 ÷ 14 = 240, so 240 caps were sold in total. So, looking at the graph, it appears that about half of the caps were white, around 120. The graph also shows that the other 3 colors were sold in about equal numbers, so dividing the other half, 120, by 3, gives around 40. Then, adding 120 white caps and 40 pink caps, gives an answer of 160. The club had close to 160 combined sales of white and pink caps.

30. B: First add all of the lengths together to get $43\frac{1}{2}$ inches. Then divide by 6 to get the mean. $43\frac{1}{2} \div 6 = 7\frac{1}{4}$

31. D: This procedure first finds the area to be fertilized, by multiplying the length and width of the rectangular yard. Then, it divides that area by the area each pound of fertilizer will cover.

32. D: $380 is 80% of $475, and answer choice D is the only one that represents this. s=.8r

33. 24: Begin by arranging the different weights from least to greatest:
48 lbs, 55 lbs, 61 lbs, 63 lbs 68 lbs, 72 lbs. Range is the difference between the highest and lowest values in a set of data; therefore, 72 – 48 = 24.

34. 6: To find the greatest common factor first factor both numbers completely. The factors of 66 include 1, 2, 3, 6, 11, 22, 33, and 66. The factors of 24 include 1, 2, 3, 4, 6, 8, 12, and 24. The greatest factor that they have in common is 6.

35. B: After the reflection and the translation the new point would be here:

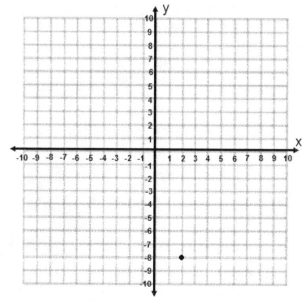

and that is the point (2, -8)

36. C: It is easier to think as the required 16 inches as 16.00 and convert all answer choices to a decimal to compare. Anything greater than 16.00 would be sufficient. $15\frac{7}{10}$ is equal to 15.7, $\frac{47}{3}$ is equivalent to 15.67 and 15.5 remains 15.5. These three choices are all slightly less than the required 16.00 inches; therefore making 16.25 inches the only adequate choice.

37. C: Since she earns $5 for walking dogs and watering flowers, this term can be combined to simplify the equation. The other terms for bringing back trashcans and checking the mail are straight multiplication.

38. A: To correctly write a percent as a decimal, the percent sign is dropped and the number is rewritten with the decimal point two places to the left. If there is not two digits in the percent, a zero is used as a place holder. This is because a percent is always a value out of 100 and the second place after the decimal point is the hundredths place. So, 8% = 0.08.

39. D: Each of the units represents $\frac{1}{4}$. The point Z is 9 units right of the y-axis or $\frac{9}{4}$ units, which is equivalent to $2\frac{1}{4}$. The point R is also 9 units from the y-axis, or $\frac{9}{4}$, which is equivalent to $2\frac{1}{4}$. Be careful to notice that coordinate pairs always come in the order of the x-coordinate and then the y-coordinate, and is defined by the pair of numbers. The y-coordinate for Z is $\frac{7}{8}$, while Point R has a y-coordinate of $3\frac{1}{2}$.

40. Part A: Count the number of customers in each age group and draw a bar on the histogram that represents that.

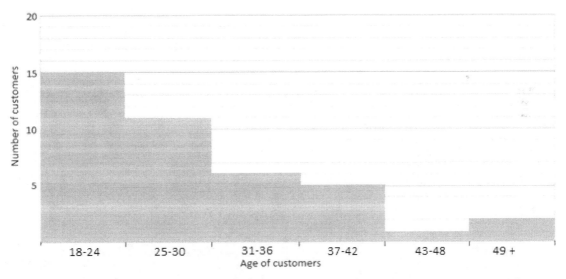

Part B: Yes: The median is the middle number of the group. Since there are 40 numbers there is no middle number so the median is the mean of the 20th and 21st number. Since this problem does not ask for a specific number there is no reason to write out the numbers and find the 20th and 21st. Instead you can see that the 25-30 age range encompasses numbers 16-26, so yes the median is in that range.

Practice Test #2

Practice Questions

1. Four students measured the length of the pencil each was using. The list shows the lengths, in centimeters, of the four pencils.
      17.03 cm, 17.4 cm, 17.31 cm, 17.09 cm
Which list shows the lengths of the pencils in order, from shortest to longest?

   Ⓐ 17.4 cm, 17.31 cm, 17.09 cm, 17.03 cm

   Ⓑ 17.03 cm, 17.09 cm, 17.4 cm, 17.31 cm

   Ⓒ 17.4 cm, 17.03 cm, 17.09 cm, 17.31 cm

   Ⓓ 17.03 cm, 17.09 cm, 17.31 cm, 17.4 cm

2. Castor collects only baseball and football cards. He has 40 baseball cards and 10 football cards. Which decimal best shows the part of his entire card collection represented by his baseball cards?

   Ⓐ 0.8

   Ⓑ 0.75

   Ⓒ 0.4

   Ⓓ 0.25

3. Which expression best shows the prime factorization of 630?

   Ⓐ $2 \times 3 \times 105$

   Ⓑ $2 \times 5 \times 7 \times 9$

   Ⓒ $2 \times 3^2 \times 5 \times 7$

   Ⓓ $2^2 \times 3^2 \times 5 \times 7$

4. Place the following numbers on the number line in the correct location:
$$-\frac{5}{3}, -\frac{2}{5}, 1.3, 1\frac{3}{5}$$

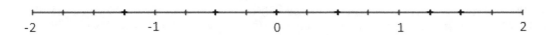

5. A club is making necklaces in school colors. They plan to use an equal number of blue beads and silver beads on each necklace. The blue beads come in bags of 60 and the silver beads come in bags of 80. What is the smallest number of bags of each color the club can purchase to have an equal number of each color bead with no beads left when the necklaces are finished?

Ⓐ 3 bags of blue and 4 bags of silver

Ⓑ 4 bags of blue and 3 bags of silver

Ⓒ 40 bags of blue and 30 bags of silver

Ⓓ 80 bags of blue and 60 bags of silver

6. Evan measured the amount of rain in the gauge over the weekend. On Saturday, he measured $1\frac{6}{10}$ inches and on Sunday, $\frac{8}{10}$ inches. What is the total amount of rain, in inches, Evan measured on those two days, written in the simplest form?

Ⓐ $1\frac{14}{20}$

Ⓑ $1\frac{4}{10}$

Ⓒ $1\frac{2}{5}$

Ⓓ $2\frac{2}{5}$

7. Rafael purchased 8 new tires for the two family cars. The price of each tire was $144, including taxes. He agreed to make 18 equal monthly payments, interest-free, to pay for the tires. What will be the amount Rafael should pay each month?

Ⓐ $16

Ⓑ $32

Ⓒ $64

Ⓓ $128

8. Part A: In the graph below what is the area of the smaller figure? Each square on the graph is one square unit.

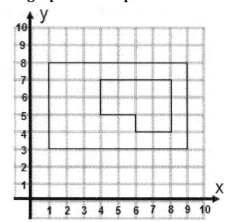

Part B: The area of the smaller figure is what fraction of the larger one?

9. William needs to find the value of the expression below. What is the value of this expression? $3^2 \times 2 - 4(3 - 1)$

Ⓐ 28

Ⓑ 18

Ⓒ 14

Ⓓ 10

10. Elena counted the number of birds that came to her bird bath one afternoon. While she watched, 20 sparrows, 16 finches, 4 wrens, and 10 jays came to the bird bath. Which ratio, in simplest form, compares the number of finches that Elena counted to the number of sparrows?

Ⓐ 4 : 5

Ⓑ 4 : 9

Ⓒ 16 : 20

Ⓓ 20 : 36

11. One cold afternoon at a small café, 20 people drank hot tea, 45 drank coffee, and 15 drank hot chocolate. Which ratio compares the number of people who drank coffee to the number who drank tea?

Ⓐ 4 to 13

Ⓑ 4 to 9

Ⓒ 9 to 4

Ⓓ 3 to 1

12. Part A: A lake near Armando's home is reported to be 80% full of water. Which fraction is equivalent to 80% and in simplest form?

Ⓐ $\frac{1}{80}$

Ⓑ $\frac{8}{10}$

Ⓒ $\frac{4}{5}$

Ⓓ $\frac{80}{1}$

Part B: If the lake is currently 12 feet deep, how deep would it be when it is completely full?

13. The rectangle in this drawing is divided into equal-sized parts, with some of them shaded a darker color.

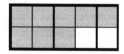

What percent best represents the part of the rectangle that is shaded a darker color?

Ⓐ 8%

Ⓑ 20%

Ⓒ 53%

Ⓓ 80%

14. Annette read that out of 20 televisions sold in her state last year, 3 were Brand V. If a furniture store near her home sold 360 televisions last year, about how many should Annette expect to be Brand V?

Ⓐ 18

Ⓑ 54

Ⓒ 1,080

Ⓓ 2,400

15. Thomas has mapped out his neighborhood on the graph below. He marked his house with the Point H, he marked his school with the point S, and he marked the park with the point P. Each square on the graph represents 0.25 miles. In the morning he walks to school, and after school he walks to the park. How far has he walked?

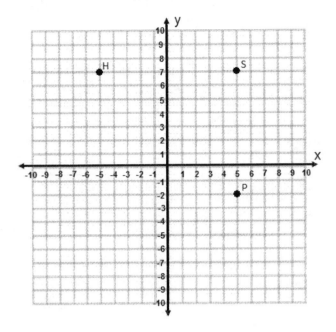

16. The table below gives the positions of several terms in a sequence and the values of those terms.

Sequence

Position of term, n	Value of Term
1	1
2	6
3	11
4	16
5	21
n	?

Which rule can be used to find the value of n?

(A) 5n

(B) 6n

(C) 5n − 4

(D) 6n − 5

- 89 -

17. Julia has a cell phone contract with a monthly charge of $45. She bought a phone with a one-time price of $50 with that contract. Which table best represents the total of all charges which should be paid at the end of each month of the contract?

Ⓐ

Number of Months	1	2	3	4	5	6
Total Charges	$45	$90	$135	$180	$225	$270

Ⓑ

Number of Months	1	2	3	4	5	6
Total Charges	$95	$140	$185	$230	$275	$320

Ⓒ

Number of Months	1	2	3	4	5	6
Total Charges	$95	$190	$285	$380	$475	$570

Ⓓ

Number of Months	1	2	3	4	5	6
Total Charges	$50	$95	$140	$185	$230	$275

18. This table shows bases, heights, and areas of four triangles. In each triangle, the base remains the same and the height changes.

Triangles

Base, b	30 yards	30 yards	30 yards	30 yards
Height, h	20 yards	40 yards	60 yards	80 yards
Area, A	300 square yards	600 square yards	900 square yards	1200 square yards

Which formula best represents the relationship between A, the areas of these triangles, and h, their heights?

Ⓐ $A = \dfrac{h}{30}$

Ⓑ $A = \dfrac{h}{15}$

Ⓒ $A = 30h$

Ⓓ $A = 15h$

19. An automobile mechanic charges $65 per hour when repairing an automobile. There is also a charge for the parts required. Which equation can the mechanic use to calculate the charge, *c*, to repair an automobile which requires *h* hours and *p* dollars worth of parts?

Ⓐ $c = 65(h + p)$

Ⓑ $c = 65h + p$

Ⓒ $c = 65p + h$

Ⓓ $c = h + p$

20. Greg knows that in the triangle below, $m\angle X$ is 50° more than $m\angle V$.

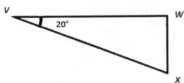

What is the measure of $\angle W$?

Ⓐ 20°

Ⓑ 50°

Ⓒ 70°

Ⓓ 90°

21. Silvia knows that in this shape, $\angle M$ is equal in measure to $\angle K$, and that the measure of $\angle N$ is 4 times the measure of $\angle K$.

What is the measure of $\angle L$?

Ⓐ 36°

Ⓑ 72°

Ⓒ 144°

Ⓓ 288°

22. There are five points labeled on this grid.

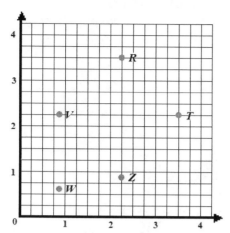

Which of the points on the grid best represents the point at $(3\frac{1}{2}, 2\frac{1}{4})$?

Ⓐ R

Ⓑ T

Ⓒ V

Ⓓ W

23. Curtis measured the temperature of water in a flask in Science class. The temperature of the water was 35°C. He carefully heated the flask so that the temperature of the water increased about 2°C every 3 minutes. About how much had the temperature of the water increased after 20 minutes?

Ⓐ 10°C

Ⓑ 15°C

Ⓒ 35°C

Ⓓ 50°C

24. Carlos helped in the library by putting new books on the shelves. Each shelf held between 21 and 24 books. Each bookcase had 5 shelves and Carlos filled 2 of the bookcases. Which number is nearest to the number of books Carlos put on the shelves?

Ⓐ 100

Ⓑ 195

Ⓒ 215

Ⓓ 240

25. Several angles and a protractor are shown in this drawing.

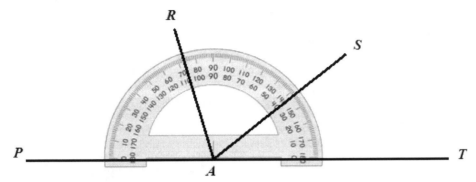

Which measure, in degrees, is closest to the measure of ∠PAS?

Ⓐ 37°

Ⓑ 43°

Ⓒ 143°

Ⓓ 157°

26. A lamp Sara decided to order online comes in four colors: brown, tan, white, and yellow. The shade for the lamp can be one of two styles: round or square. Which list shows all the possible combinations for a lamp of one color and one style for its shade that Sara can order?

Ⓐ Brown, round   White, square

 Tan, round   Yellow, square

Ⓑ Brown, tan   Yellow, round

 Tan, white   Round, square
 White, yellow

Ⓒ Brown, tan   Tan, white

 Brown, white   Tan, round
 Brown, yellow Tan, square

Ⓓ Brown, round   Brown, square

 Tan, round   Tan, square
 White, round   White, square
 Yellow, round Yellow, square

- 93 -

27. Alma collected coins. In the bag where she kept only dimes, she had dimes from four different years. She had 20 dimes minted in 1942, 30 minted in 1943, 40 minted in 1944, and 10 minted in 1945. If Alma reached into the bag without looking and took a dime, what is the probability that she took a dime minted in 1945?

Ⓐ $\frac{2}{5}$

Ⓑ $\frac{3}{10}$

Ⓒ $\frac{1}{5}$

Ⓓ $\frac{1}{10}$

28. Jacob recorded the high temperature in his backyard each day for six days. The list below shows those high temperatures.

61°, 54°, 58°, 63°, 71°, 71°

Which of these temperatures is the median of the ones in Jacob's list?

Ⓐ 17°

Ⓑ 62°

Ⓒ 63°

Ⓓ 71°

29. Mr. Smith paid $60 for a kit to build a dollhouse for his granddaughter. He also paid $10 for tools, $20 for paint, and $10 for other supplies to build the dollhouse. Which graph best represents the dollhouse expenses Mr. Smith had?

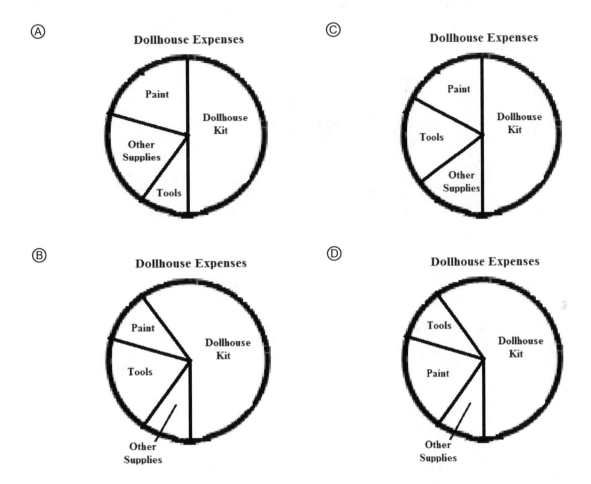

30. People who attended an orchestra concert at Johnson Middle School were asked to which of five age groups they belonged. The data is recorded in this graph.

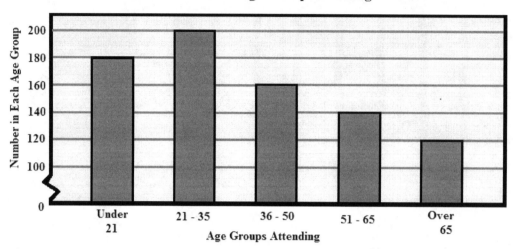

Which table correctly represents the data recorded in the graph?

Ⓐ

Number of Each Age Group Attending Concert

Age Group (in years)	Under 21	21 – 35	36 – 50	51 – 65	Over 65
Number in Group	180	200	160	140	120

Ⓑ

Number of Each Age Group Attending Concert

Age Group (in years)	Under 21	21 – 35	36 – 50	51 – 65	Over 65
Number in Group	180	220	180	160	140

Ⓒ

Number of Each Age Group Attending Concert

Age Group (in years)	Under 21	21 – 35	36 – 50	51 – 65	Over 65
Number in Group	180	200	140	120	100

Ⓓ

Number of Each Age Group Attending Concert

Age Group (in years)	Under 21	21 – 35	36 – 50	51 – 65	Over 65
Number in Group	180	200	160	120	120

31. Harlan plans to make stew for a large group. The recipe he uses requires 150 carrots. He knows that he can buy large bags of carrots for $3.75 each. What additional information does Harlan need to find the amount of money the carrots will cost for his stew?

Ⓐ The amounts of other vegetables he will need for the stew

Ⓑ The number of people he expects to eat the stew

Ⓒ The price each person attending the event paid

Ⓓ The number of carrots in a large bag of carrots

32. The cashier at Weekender Video Arcade recorded the number of tokens sold on Thursday, Friday, Saturday, and Sunday during one weekend. The graph shows the number of tokens sold on each of those four days.

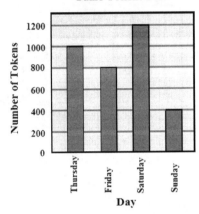

If the tokens sell for $1.25, what amount of money should the cashier have received for tokens sold on Friday and Saturday combined?

Ⓐ $1,500

Ⓑ $2,000

Ⓒ $2,500

Ⓓ $2,250

33. Part A: It took Hailey 18 minutes to jog from her house to the park. If the park is 2.5 miles away how long did it take her to go 1 mile?

_____

_____

_____

Part B: If she keeps the same pace how long will it take her to go from the park to her friend's house that is 3.5 miles away?

_____

_____

_____

34. Mr. Foster wants to put new carpet on the floor of his rectangular playroom. The playroom is 27 feet long and 18 feet wide. He has found an inexpensive carpet that is priced $14 per square yard. What would be a reasonable price for enough carpet to cover the floor of his playroom?

Ⓐ $486

Ⓑ $756

Ⓒ $1,260

Ⓓ $2,268

35. The rectangular floor of a garage has an area of 198 square feet. Andy knows that the floor is 7 feet longer than it is wide. What is length of the floor of the garage?

Ⓐ 11 feet

Ⓑ 14 feet

Ⓒ 18 feet

Ⓓ 92 feet

36. Timothy brought 12 of his toy cars to the baby sitters. These toy cars represent 30% of his toy car collection. What is the total number of cars in Timothy's collection? Show your work.

_____

_____

_____

37. Kenneth needs to repaint a wall in his bathroom. The wall is 8 feet high and 14 feet long. Part of the wall is covered with tile and he will not paint that part. The part of the wall covered by tile is 14 feet long and 42 inches high. Which expression could Kenneth use to find the area of the part of the wall he needs to repaint?

Ⓐ $14 \times 8 - (42 + 8)$

Ⓑ $14 \times 8 - (42 \times 14)$

Ⓒ $14 \times 8 - [(42 \div 12) \times 14]$

Ⓓ $2(14 + 8) - [(42 \div 12) + 14]$

38. Arlene had a garden for flowers. The rectangular garden was 10 feet wide and 16 feet long. In the garden, she planted daisies in a rectangular plot 5 feet wide and 10 feet long. She also planted pansies in a square plot 6 feet on each side. If Arlene planted no other flowers, how much area in her garden could still be planted?

Ⓐ 13 square feet, because $2(10 + 16) - [2(5 + 10) + 2(6 + 6)] = 13$

Ⓑ 38 square feet, because $2(10 + 16) - (5 \times 10) + (6 \times 6) = 38$

Ⓒ 74 square feet, because $10 \times 16 - [(5 \times 10) + (6 \times 6)] = 74$

Ⓓ 146 square feet, because $10 \times 16 - (5 \times 100) + (6 \times 6) = 146$

39. There are five points labeled on this grid.

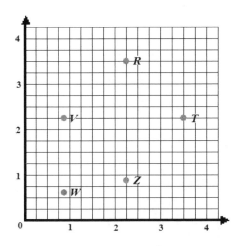

Which of the coordinates on the grid best represents the point R?

Ⓐ $(3\frac{1}{2}, 2\frac{1}{2})$

Ⓑ $(2\frac{1}{4}, 3\frac{1}{2})$

Ⓒ $(3\frac{1}{2}, 4\frac{1}{2})$

Ⓓ $(2\frac{1}{4}, 3\frac{1}{4})$

- 99 -

40. A fair was open for 4 days. The attendance to the fair during those 4 days is recorded below as well as the number of ride tickets sold.

Day	Number of entrants	Number of tickets sold
1	102	510
2	114	912
3	108	756
4	131	1048

Part A: How many tickets were sold per entrant on day 2?

Part B: What is the average number of tickets sold per entrant over the entire 4 day?

Answers and Explanations

1. D: To correctly order the numbers in this question, making the decimals all have the same number of digits by adding as many zeros as necessary to the numbers with fewer digits makes them easier to compare. Here, only 17.4 has fewer digits than the others, so add one zero to make it 17.40 (*this does not change the value*). Now, by comparing place values from left to right of 17.03, 17.4, 17.31, and 17.09, we see that 17.03 is the shortest, 17.09 is the next longest, 17.31 is the third longest, and 17.4 is the longest. Notice the question asked for shortest to longest, not longest to shortest.

2. A: In order to answer this question, we add the number of baseball and football cards to realize that there are 50 total cards in Castor's collection, 40 of which are baseball cards. To convert this to a decimal, we need to divide 40 by 50. This gives the correct answer, 0.8.

3. C: There is more than one way to solve this problem. One method is to use the fact that the number ends in 0. This means 10 is a factor. So, 10 × 63 = 630. 10 has prime factors of 2 and 5. 63 has factors of 7 and 9 and the 9 has two factors of 3. Putting the prime factors in order, least to greatest, and showing the two factors of 3 with an exponent of 2 gives us the answer: $2 \times 3^2 \times 5 \times 7$.

4. $-\frac{5}{3}$ is going to be slightly more than the $-1\frac{3}{4}$ mark on the number line. $-\frac{2}{5}$ is going to be a little more than $-\frac{1}{2}$ mark. 1.3 is going to be a little more than the $1\frac{1}{4}$ mark. $1\frac{3}{5}$ is going to be a little more than the $1\frac{3}{4}$ mark.

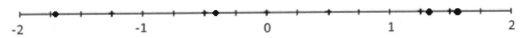

5. B: There is more than one way to solve this problem. One method is to find the least common multiple of 60 and 80. To do this, first find the prime factors of each number.
60 = 2 × 2 × 3 × 5
80 = 2 × 2 × 2 × 2 × 5
The factors common to 60 and 80 are 2, 2, and 5. The factors that are not common to both numbers are two factors of 2 from 80 and a factor of 3 from 60. To find the least common multiple, multiply all the factors without repetition. That is, multiply the common factors (2, 2, and 5) and the other factors (2, 2, and 3) together:
2 × 2 × 2 × 2 × 3 × 5 = 240
240 is the least common multiple. This is the total number of beads needed of each color. To find how many bags the club will need to purchase, divide this total by the number of beads that come in each bag for each color bead. 240 ÷ 60 = 4 (4 bags of blue). 240 ÷ 80 = 3 (3 bags of silver).

6. D: To answer this question, note that the fractions have common denominators. When adding fractions with common denominators, we need to add only the numerators, so, the sum of $\frac{6}{10}$ and $\frac{8}{10}$ is $\frac{14}{10}$. This should then be written as a mixed number, $1\frac{4}{10}$, which is found by dividing 14 by 10 which gives the whole number and the remainder becomes your new numerator over the same denominator of 10. The fraction $\frac{4}{10}$ can also be written as $\frac{2}{5}$ by dividing numerator and denominator by the common factor of 2. Therefore, $\frac{14}{10}$ is equivalent to $1\frac{2}{5}$. Be careful here to remember the 1 from the original $1\frac{6}{10}$ amount given in the problem, which must be added to the $1\frac{2}{5}$ to make a total of $2\frac{2}{5}$.

7. C: First, multiply the cost of each tire, \$144, by the number of tires, 8, to get \$1,152. Then, divide \$1,152 by the number of months, 18, to get the amount paid each month, \$64.

8. Part A: 10: The number of square units inside the figure is 10.

Part B: $\frac{1}{4}$: The larger figure is 8 by 5 so it is 40 square units. So, it is $\frac{10}{40} = \frac{1}{4}$.

9. D: To simplify this expression, use the order of operations.
$$3^2 \times 2 - 4(3 - 1)$$
$$= 3^2 \times 2 - 4(2)$$
$$= 9 \times 2 - 4(2)$$
$$= 18 - 8$$
$$= 10$$

10. A: The ratio asked for is the number of finches compared to the number of sparrows. This compares 16 to 20, but the ratio can be written in simpler form by dividing both numbers in the ratio by 4, to get the ratio of 4 to 5. It is important to notice the order of the ratio. Since the number of finches is written before the number of sparrows, the ratio must be 16 to 20 and not 20 to 16. Also, note that the number of wrens or jays does not matter here.

11. C: The ratio compares the number of coffee drinkers to the number of tea drinkers, in that order, so the ratio is 45 to 20. Note that the ratio of 20 to 45 would be incorrect. The ratio of 45 to 20 can then be written in simpler terms by dividing both terms by 5 to get 9 to 4. Notice that the number of hot chocolate drinkers is not important in this problem.

12. Part A: C: The 80% means 80 out of 100, which can be written as $\frac{80}{100}$. This fraction can be written in lowest terms by dividing both the numerator and denominator by the greatest common factor of 20, to get the fraction, $\frac{4}{5}$.

Part B: 15 feet: If the lake is 12 feet deep at 80% full then you can just divide 12 by .8 to get 15 feet.

13. D: The number of shaded parts is 8 and the total number of parts is 10. This can be written as the ratio: $\frac{8}{10}$. Since percent is always a ratio with a denominator of 100, multiply both terms of the ratio by 10 to get the ratio: $\frac{80}{100}$, which can be written as 80%.

14. B: One method that can be used to answer this question is to write and solve the proportion: $\frac{3}{20} = \frac{V}{360}$, where V stands for the number of Brand V televisions that were sold at the furniture store. To solve the proportion, we can cross multiply: 20 times V and 3 times 360, which gives the equation: $20V = 1,080$. We solve this equation by dividing both sides of the equation by 20 to get $V = 54$.

15. 4.75: Point H is located at (-5, 7), and Point S is located at (5, 7). The distance between these is 10 units on the graph or 2.5 miles. Point P is located at (5, -2). The distance between it and Point S is 9 units on the graph or 2.25 miles. So, Thomas walked a total of 4.75 miles.

16. C: Notice that there is a difference of 5 between the values in Column 2. This gives the "5" in front of *n*. Then, notice that if you multiply the position of the term by 5, the value is less than that product, by 4. So, the rule is $5n - 4$.

17. B: There is a one-time charge of $50 for the price of the phone and a $45 monthly charge in the first month for a total of $95. Then, a charge of $45 only is added for every month after that. Since the chart shows the total charge each month, adding $45 to the total due from the first month gives a total of $140 for the first 2 months. Then, $45 is added for the next month, for a total of $185 for the first 3 months, $230 for 4 months, $275 for 5 months, and $320 in total charges for the first 6 months.

18. D: The formula for the area of a triangle can be used here, but it is not necessary. To find the relationship between the heights and areas, look at the last two rows. A pattern can be seen that each value for the area, *A*, is just 15 times the value of the height, *h*. So, the formula is: $A = 15h$.

19. B: The amount charged for hours worked will require us to multiply the number of hours by $65. The charge for parts is not changed by the number of hours worked. So, the equation needs to show 65 times *h*, the number of hours, plus *p*, the price of the parts. So, the correct equation is: $c = 65h + p$.

20. D: To find $m\angle W$, we must first find the measure of $\angle X$. We know $m\angle X$ is 50° more than $m\angle V$. Since $m\angle V = 20°$, then $m\angle X = 20° + 50° = 70°$. So, $m\angle V + m\angle X = 90°$. It is important here to know that the sum of the three angles of any triangle is 180°. Since $m\angle V + m\angle X = 90°$, then $90° + m\angle W = 180°$. So, $m\angle W = 90°$.

21. C: Since we are told that $m\angle N$ is 4 times $m\angle K$, we can find the $m\angle N$ by multiplying 36° by 4 to get 144°. Knowing $\angle M$ measures 36° because it is equal to $m\angle K$ gives us the measures of three of the angles. The sum of the four angles of a quadrilateral always equals 360°. So, we add the measures of the three angles that we know and then subtract that total from 360°:
360 – (36 + 144 + 36) = 360 – 216 = 144. The measure of $\angle L$ is 144°.

22. B: Each of the units represents $\frac{1}{4}$. The point *T* is 14 units right of the *y*-axis or $\frac{14}{4}$ units, which is equivalent to $3\frac{1}{2}$. The point *T* is also 9 units from the *x*-axis, or $\frac{9}{4}$, which is equivalent to $2\frac{1}{4}$. Be careful to notice that coordinate pairs always come in the order of the *x*-coordinate and then the *y*-coordinate, which is why Point *R* would be incorrect.

23. B: Since the water temperature increased by about 2° every 3 minutes, we need to divide the total time of 20 minutes by 3 minutes, which is about 7. This means the temperature was raised about 7 times. Then we need to multiply 7 by 2, since the temperature went up by 2° each time. So, the temperature goes up by about 14° total. Since the problem asks for the increase in temperature and not the total temperature that results after the increases, 15 is the closest to our answer.

24. C: First, since there are 5 shelves on each of the 2 bookcases, we multiply 5 by 2 to get 10 shelves total. Then, we find the minimum and maximum number of books that could have filled the shelves. Since 21 times 10 is 210 and 24 times 10 is 240, The number of books he shelved must be between 210 and 240. Answer D is 240, which would mean that every shelf was filled with the maximum number of books, which is not as likely.

25. C: Since segment PA lies along the left side of the protractor, we should read the outside scale. The segment SA passes between 140° and 150°, much closer to 140°, so the correct answer is 143°.

26. D: This list is the only one which lists all the possible ways Sara can order the lamp. Each of the four color choices can be chosen, and they can all be combined with one of two styles. In total, there are eight possibilities.

27. D: By adding all of the dimes, we find that there are a total of 100 dimes in the bag. 10 of them were minted in 1945. The probability, then, of choosing a dime minted in 1945 is 10 out of 100, which is equivalent to the fraction $\frac{1}{10}$.

28. B: To find the median of a set of data, first arrange the numbers in numerical order. Since this is an even numbered list, the two most central numbers are 61 and 63. Midway between these numbers is 62.

29. D: By adding up all of Mr. Smith's expenses for the dollhouse, $60 + $10 + $20 + $10, you find that his expenses totaled $100. Mr. Smith spent $60 on the kit, which is more than $\frac{1}{2}$ his expenses ($\frac{1}{2}$ of $100 would be $50), $\frac{1}{10}$ of his expenses on tools ($\frac{1}{10}$ of $100 = $10), $\frac{1}{5}$ of his expenses on paint ($\frac{1}{5}$ of $100 = $20), and $\frac{1}{10}$ of his expenses on other supplies. This is the only graph that correctly shows these fractions.

30. A: This table is the only one with the correct numbers from the graph for each category.

31. D: Since Harlan knows the cost of each bag of carrots, and also how many total carrots he needs, he also needs to know the number of carrots in each bag to find the number of bags he needs to buy. Then, he can multiply the number of bags by the price to find the amount of money the carrots for his stew will cost.

32. C: Though the graph shows the numbers of tokens sold on Thursday through Sunday, we are only asked about those sold on Friday and Saturday. So, we add those numbers together to get 800 + 1,200 = 2,000. Then, since each of the 2,000 tokens sold for $1.25 each, the 2,000 should be multiplied by $1.25 to get $2500.

33. Part A: 7.2 minutes: If it takes her 18 minutes to jog 2.5 miles then just divide 18 by 2.5 to get 7.2 minutes.

Part B: 25.2 minutes: If she keeps the same pace then it would take her 7.2 minutes times 3.5 miles. This equals 25.2 minutes.

34. B: It is necessary to find the area of the floor by multiplying the dimensions together. However, since the dimensions are given in feet and we only know the price of carpeting per square yard, converting the dimensions from feet to yards first is helpful. Since there are 3 feet in a yard, dividing each of the dimensions by 3 will give us the measurements in yards. So, 18/3 = 6 and 27/3 = 9. So, the floor is 6 yards by 9 yards, which is an area of 54 square yards. Last, we multiply 54 by $14, since each square yard costs $14 and there are 54, so the price of the carpet should be $756.

35. C: Guess and check is one way to find the correct answer. We know the length times the width gives the area of the garage floor, 198 square feet. We might guess that the width is 9. We know that the length is 7 more than the width, so, then the length would be 16. 9 times 16 is 144. We would see that our first guess is too low, so we guess higher. We might guess 12 for the width. The length is 7 more, so the length would be 19. 12 times 19 is 228, but this is too high. When we try 11 for the width, we find the length to be 18. 11 times 18 is 198, so the width of the garage floor is 11 and the length is 18. Be careful to note that the question asks for the length and not the width.

36. 40: If 12 of his cars represents 30% of his collection the divide by 3 to find 10% and then multiply by 10 to get 100%. $12 \div 3 = 4 \times 10 = 40$.

37. C: We multiply the length and wide of the wall to find the area of the entire wall. So, 8 × 14. Then, we want to subtract the area of the tiled section that does not need to be painted from the area of the entire wall. However, the height of the tiled section is given in inches, while all the other dimensions in the problem are given in feet. So, we must convert this to feet. Since we are going from a smaller unit to a larger unit (inches to feet), we want to divide. We need to divide 42 by 12 since that is the conversion factor (12 inches in 1 foot). Then we multiply the height (in feet) by the length to find the area covered by the tile. So, this is 14 times the 42 divided by 12. Last, we subtract the two areas to find the area of the part of the wall Kenneth will repaint.

38. C: The area of the garden should be found by multiplying 10 times 16 to get 160. Then the area of the daisy plot can be found by multiplying 5 times 10 to get 50, and the area of the pansy plot can be found by multiplying 6 times 6 to get 36. We then add the 50 square feet and 36 square feet to get 86 square feet, which is the area the two plots (daisy and pansy) cover. To find the area of the garden that can still be planted, subtract that from the total area of 160 square feet to get 74 square feet.

39. B: Each of the units represents $\frac{1}{4}$. The point R is 9 units to the right of the y-axis or $\frac{9}{4}$, which is equivalent to $2\frac{1}{4}$. Point R is also 14 units above the x-axis or $\frac{14}{4}$, which is equivalent to $3\frac{1}{2}$. Be careful to notice that coordinate pairs always come in the order of the x-coordinate and then the y-coordinate.

40. D: Only answer D correctly shows each amount of birdfeed being subtracted from the original total amount of 10 cups that originally given to Xander.

Success Strategies

The most important thing you can do is to ignore your fears and jump into the test immediately. Do not be overwhelmed by any strange-sounding terms. You have to jump into the test like jumping into a pool—all at once is the easiest way.

Make Predictions

As you read and understand the question, try to guess what the answer will be. Remember that several of the answer choices are wrong, and once you begin reading them, your mind will immediately become cluttered with answer choices designed to throw you off. Your mind is typically the most focused immediately after you have read the question and digested its contents. If you can, try to predict what the correct answer will be. You may be surprised at what you can predict.

Quickly scan the choices and see if your prediction is in the listed answer choices. If it is, then you can be quite confident that you have the right answer. It still won't hurt to check the other answer choices, but most of the time, you've got it!

Answer the Question

It may seem obvious to only pick answer choices that answer the question, but the test writers can create some excellent answer choices that are wrong. Don't pick an answer just because it sounds right, or you believe it to be true. It MUST answer the question. Once you've made your selection, always go back and check it against the question and make sure that you didn't misread the question and that the answer choice does answer the question posed.

Benchmark

After you read the first answer choice, decide if you think it sounds correct or not. If it doesn't, move on to the next answer choice. If it does, mentally mark that answer choice. This doesn't mean that you've definitely selected it as your answer choice, it just means that it's the best you've seen thus far. Go ahead and read the next choice. If the next choice is worse than the one you've already selected, keep going to the next answer choice. If the next choice is better than the choice you've already selected, mentally mark the new answer choice as your best guess.

The first answer choice that you select becomes your standard. Every other answer choice must be benchmarked against that standard. That choice is correct until proven otherwise by another answer choice beating it out. Once you've decided that no other answer choice seems as good, do one final check to ensure that your answer choice answers the question posed.

Valid Information

Don't discount any of the information provided in the question. Every piece of information may be necessary to determine the correct answer. None of the information in the question is there to throw you off (while the answer choices will certainly have information to throw you off). If two seemingly unrelated topics are discussed, don't ignore either. You can be confident there is a relationship, or it wouldn't be included in the question, and you are probably going to have to determine what is that relationship to find the answer.

Avoid "Fact Traps"

Don't get distracted by a choice that is factually true. Your search is for the answer that answers the question. Stay focused and don't fall for an answer that is true but irrelevant. Always go back to the question and make sure you're choosing an answer that actually answers the question and is not just a true statement. An answer can be factually correct, but it MUST answer the question asked. Additionally, two answers can both be seemingly correct, so be sure to read all of the answer choices, and make sure that you get the one that BEST answers the question.

Milk the Question

Some of the questions may throw you completely off. They might deal with a subject you have not been exposed to, or one that you haven't reviewed in years. While your lack of knowledge about the subject will be a hindrance, the question itself can give you many clues that will help you find the correct answer. Read the question carefully and look for clues. Watch particularly for adjectives and nouns describing difficult terms or words that you don't recognize. Regardless of whether you completely understand a word or not, replacing it with a synonym, either provided or one you more familiar with, may help you to understand what the questions are asking. Rather than wracking your mind about specific detailed information concerning a difficult term or word, try to use mental substitutes that are easier to understand.

The Trap of Familiarity

Don't just choose a word because you recognize it. On difficult questions, you may not recognize a number of words in the answer choices. The test writers don't put "make-believe" words on the test, so don't think that just because you only recognize all the words in one answer choice that that answer choice must be correct. If you only recognize words in one answer choice, then focus on that one. Is it correct? Try your best to determine if it is correct. If it is, that's great. If not, eliminate it. Each word and answer choice you eliminate increases your chances of getting the question correct, even if you then have to guess among the unfamiliar choices.

Eliminate Answers

Eliminate choices as soon as you realize they are wrong. But be careful! Make sure you consider all of the possible answer choices. Just because one appears right, doesn't mean that the next one won't be even better! The test writers will usually put more than one good answer choice for every question, so read all of them. Don't worry if you are stuck between two that seem right. By getting down to just two remaining possible choices, your odds are now 50/50. Rather than wasting too much time, play the odds. You are guessing, but guessing wisely because you've been able to knock out some of the answer choices that you know are wrong. If you are eliminating choices and realize that the last answer choice you are left with is also obviously wrong, don't panic. Start over and consider each choice again. There may easily be something that you missed the first time and will realize on the second pass.

Tough Questions

If you are stumped on a problem or it appears too hard or too difficult, don't waste time. Move on! Remember though, if you can quickly check for obviously incorrect answer choices, your chances of guessing correctly are greatly improved. Before you completely give up, at least try to knock out a couple of possible answers. Eliminate what you can and then guess at the remaining answer choices before moving on.

Brainstorm

If you get stuck on a difficult question, spend a few seconds quickly brainstorming. Run through the complete list of possible answer choices. Look at each choice and ask yourself, "Could this answer the question satisfactorily?" Go through each answer choice and consider it independently of the others. By systematically going through all possibilities, you may find something that you would otherwise overlook. Remember though that when you get stuck, it's important to try to keep moving.

Read Carefully

Understand the problem. Read the question and answer choices carefully. Don't miss the question because you misread the terms. You have plenty of time to read each question thoroughly and make sure you understand what is being asked. Yet a happy medium must be attained, so don't waste too much time. You must read carefully, but efficiently.

Face Value

When in doubt, use common sense. Always accept the situation in the problem at face value. Don't read too much into it. These problems will not require you to make huge leaps of logic. The test writers aren't trying to throw you off with a cheap trick. If you have to go beyond creativity and make a leap of logic in order to have an answer choice answer the question, then you should look at the other answer choices. Don't overcomplicate the problem by creating theoretical relationships or explanations that will warp time or space. These are normal problems rooted in reality. It's just that the applicable relationship or explanation may not be readily apparent and you have to figure things out. Use your common sense to interpret anything that isn't clear.

Prefixes

If you're having trouble with a word in the question or answer choices, try dissecting it. Take advantage of every clue that the word might include. Prefixes and suffixes can be a huge help. Usually they allow you to determine a basic meaning. Pre- means before, post- means after, pro - is positive, de- is negative. From these prefixes and suffixes, you can get an idea of the general meaning of the word and try to put it into context. Beware though of any traps. Just because con- is the opposite of pro-, doesn't necessarily mean congress is the opposite of progress!

Hedge Phrases

Watch out for critical hedge phrases, led off with words such as "likely," "may," "can," "sometimes," "often," "almost," "mostly," "usually," "generally," "rarely," and "sometimes." Question writers insert these hedge phrases to cover every possibility. Often an answer choice will be wrong simply because it leaves no room for exception. Unless the situation calls for them, avoid answer choices that have definitive words like "exactly," and "always."

Switchback Words

Stay alert for "switchbacks." These are the words and phrases frequently used to alert you to shifts in thought. The most common switchback word is "but." Others include "although," "however," "nevertheless," "on the other hand," "even though," "while," "in spite of," "despite," and "regardless of."

New Information

Correct answer choices will rarely have completely new information included. Answer choices typically are straightforward reflections of the material asked about and will directly relate to the question. If a new piece of information is included in an answer choice that doesn't even seem to relate to the topic being asked about, then that answer choice is likely incorrect. All of the information needed to answer the question is usually provided for you in the question. You should not have to make guesses that are unsupported or choose answer choices that require unknown information that cannot be reasoned from what is given.

Time Management

On technical questions, don't get lost on the technical terms. Don't spend too much time on any one question. If you don't know what a term means, then odds are you aren't going to get much further since you don't have a dictionary. You should be able to immediately recognize whether or not you know a term. If you don't, work with the other clues that you have—the other answer choices and terms provided—but don't waste too much time trying to figure out a difficult term that you don't know.

Contextual Clues

Look for contextual clues. An answer can be right but not the correct answer. The contextual clues will help you find the answer that is most right and is correct. Understand the context in which a phrase or statement is made. This will help you make important distinctions.

Don't Panic

Panicking will not answer any questions for you; therefore, it isn't helpful. When you first see the question, if your mind goes blank, take a deep breath. Force yourself to mechanically go through the steps of solving the problem using the strategies you've learned.

Pace Yourself

Don't get clock fever. It's easy to be overwhelmed when you're looking at a page full of questions, your mind is full of random thoughts and feeling confused, and the clock is ticking down faster than you would like. Calm down and maintain the pace that you have set for yourself. As long as you are on track by monitoring your pace, you are guaranteed to have enough time for yourself. When you get to the last few minutes of the test, it may seem like you won't have enough time left, but if you only have as many questions as you should have left at that point, then you're right on track!

Answer Selection

The best way to pick an answer choice is to eliminate all of those that are wrong, until only one is left and confirm that is the correct answer. Sometimes though, an answer choice may immediately look right. Be careful! Take a second to make sure that the other choices are not equally obvious. Don't make a hasty mistake. There are only two times that you should stop before checking other answers. First is when you are positive that the answer choice you have selected is correct. Second is when time is almost out and you have to make a quick guess!

Check Your Work

Since you will probably not know every term listed and the answer to every question, it is important that you get credit for the ones that you do know. Don't miss any questions through careless mistakes. If at all possible, try to take a second to look back over your answer selection and make sure you've selected the correct answer choice and haven't made a costly careless mistake (such as marking an answer choice that you didn't mean to mark). The time it takes for this quick double check should more than pay for itself in caught mistakes.

Beware of Directly Quoted Answers

Sometimes an answer choice will repeat word for word a portion of the question or reference section. However, beware of such exact duplication. It may be a trap! More than likely, the correct choice will paraphrase or summarize a point, rather than being exactly the same wording.

Slang

Scientific sounding answers are better than slang ones. An answer choice that begins "To compare the outcomes..." is much more likely to be correct than one that begins "Because some people insisted..."

Extreme Statements

Avoid wild answers that throw out highly controversial ideas that are proclaimed as established fact. An answer choice that states the "process should used in certain situations, if..." is much more likely to be correct than one that states the "process should be discontinued completely." The first is a calm rational statement and doesn't even make a definitive, uncompromising stance, using a hedge word "if" to provide wiggle room, whereas the second choice is a radical idea and far more extreme.

Answer Choice Families

When you have two or more answer choices that are direct opposites or parallels, one of them is usually the correct answer. For instance, if one answer choice states "x increases" and another answer choice states "x decreases" or "y increases," then those two or three answer choices are very similar in construction and fall into the same family of answer choices. A family of answer choices consists of two or three answer choices, very similar in construction, but often with directly opposite meanings. Usually the correct answer choice will be in that family of answer choices. The "odd man out" or answer choice that doesn't seem to fit the parallel construction of the other answer choices is more likely to be incorrect.

How to Overcome Test Anxiety

The very nature of tests caters to some level of anxiety, nervousness, or tension, just as we feel for any important event that occurs in our lives. A little bit of anxiety or nervousness can be a good thing. It helps us with motivation, and makes achievement just that much sweeter. However, too much anxiety can be a problem, especially if it hinders our ability to function and perform.

"Test anxiety," is the term that refers to the emotional reactions that some test-takers experience when faced with a test or exam. Having a fear of testing and exams is based upon a rational fear, since the test-taker's performance can shape the course of an academic career. Nevertheless, experiencing excessive fear of examinations will only interfere with the test-taker's ability to perform and chance to be successful.

There are a large variety of causes that can contribute to the development and sensation of test anxiety. These include, but are not limited to, lack of preparation and worrying about issues surrounding the test.

Lack of Preparation

Lack of preparation can be identified by the following behaviors or situations:
- Not scheduling enough time to study, and therefore cramming the night before the test or exam
- Managing time poorly, to create the sensation that there is not enough time to do everything
- Failing to organize the text information in advance, so that the study material consists of the entire text and not simply the pertinent information
- Poor overall studying habits

Worrying, on the other hand, can be related to both the test taker, or many other factors around him/her that will be affected by the results of the test. These include worrying about:
- Previous performances on similar exams, or exams in general
- How friends and other students are achieving
- The negative consequences that will result from a poor grade or failure

There are three primary elements to test anxiety. Physical components, which involve the same typical bodily reactions as those to acute anxiety (to be discussed below). Emotional factors have to do with fear or panic. Mental or cognitive issues concerning attention spans and memory abilities.

Physical Signals

There are many different symptoms of test anxiety, and these are not limited to mental and emotional strain. Frequently there are a range of physical signals that will let a test taker know that he/she is suffering from test anxiety. These bodily changes can include the following:

- Perspiring
- Sweaty palms
- Wet, trembling hands
- Nausea
- Dry mouth
- A knot in the stomach
- Headache
- Faintness
- Muscle tension
- Aching shoulders, back and neck
- Rapid heart beat
- Feeling too hot/cold

To recognize the sensation of test anxiety, a test-taker should monitor him/herself for the following sensations:

- The physical distress symptoms as listed above
- Emotional sensitivity, expressing emotional feelings such as the need to cry or laugh too much, or a sensation of anger or helplessness
- A decreased ability to think, causing the test-taker to blank out or have racing thoughts that are hard to organize or control.

Though most students will feel some level of anxiety when faced with a test or exam, the majority can cope with that anxiety and maintain it at a manageable level. However, those who cannot are faced with a very real and very serious condition, which can and should be controlled for the immeasurable benefit of this sufferer.

Naturally, these sensations lead to negative results for the testing experience. The most common effects of test anxiety have to do with nervousness and mental blocking.

Nervousness

Nervousness can appear in several different levels:

- The test-taker's difficulty, or even inability to read and understand the questions on the test
- The difficulty or inability to organize thoughts to a coherent form
- The difficulty or inability to recall key words and concepts relating to the testing questions (especially essays)
- The receipt of poor grades on a test, though the test material was well known by the test taker

Conversely, a person may also experience mental blocking, which involves:

- Blanking out on test questions
- Only remembering the correct answers to the questions when the test has already finished.

Fortunately for test anxiety sufferers, beating these feelings, to a large degree, has to do with proper preparation. When a test taker has a feeling of preparedness, then anxiety will be dramatically lessened.

The first step to resolving anxiety issues is to distinguish which of the two types of anxiety are being suffered. If the anxiety is a direct result of a lack of preparation, this should be considered a normal reaction, and the anxiety level (as opposed to the test results) shouldn't be anything to worry about. However, if, when adequately prepared, the test-taker still panics, blanks out, or seems to overreact, this is not a fully rational reaction. While this can be considered normal too, there are many ways to combat and overcome these effects.

Remember that anxiety cannot be entirely eliminated, however, there are ways to minimize it, to make the anxiety easier to manage. Preparation is one of the best ways to minimize test anxiety. Therefore the following techniques are wise in order to best fight off any anxiety that may want to build.

To begin with, try to avoid cramming before a test, whenever it is possible. By trying to memorize an entire term's worth of information in one day, you'll be shocking your system, and not giving yourself a very good chance to absorb the information. This is an easy path to anxiety, so for those who suffer from test anxiety, cramming should not even be considered an option.

Instead of cramming, work throughout the semester to combine all of the material which is presented throughout the semester, and work on it gradually as the course goes by, making sure to master the main concepts first, leaving minor details for a week or so before the test.

To study for the upcoming exam, be sure to pose questions that may be on the examination, to gauge the ability to answer them by integrating the ideas from your texts, notes and lectures, as well as any supplementary readings.

If it is truly impossible to cover all of the information that was covered in that particular term, concentrate on the most important portions, that can be covered very well. Learn these concepts as best as possible, so that when the test comes, a goal can be made to use these concepts as presentations of your knowledge.

In addition to study habits, changes in attitude are critical to beating a struggle with test anxiety. In fact, an improvement of the perspective over the entire test-taking experience can actually help a test taker to enjoy studying and therefore improve the overall experience. Be certain not to overemphasize the significance of the grade - know that the result of the test is neither a reflection of self worth, nor is it a measure of intelligence; one grade will not predict a person's future success.

To improve an overall testing outlook, the following steps should be tried:
- Keeping in mind that the most reasonable expectation for taking a test is to expect to try to demonstrate as much of what you know as you possibly can.
- Reminding ourselves that a test is only one test; this is not the only one, and there will be others.
- The thought of thinking of oneself in an irrational, all-or-nothing term should be avoided at all costs.

- A reward should be designated for after the test, so there's something to look forward to. Whether it be going to a movie, going out to eat, or simply visiting friends, schedule it in advance, and do it no matter what result is expected on the exam.

Test-takers should also keep in mind that the basics are some of the most important things, even beyond anti-anxiety techniques and studying. Never neglect the basic social, emotional and biological needs, in order to try to absorb information. In order to best achieve, these three factors must be held as just as important as the studying itself.

Study Steps

Remember the following important steps for studying:
- Maintain healthy nutrition and exercise habits. Continue both your recreational activities and social pass times. These both contribute to your physical and emotional well being.
- Be certain to get a good amount of sleep, especially the night before the test, because when you're overtired you are not able to perform to the best of your best ability.
- Keep the studying pace to a moderate level by taking breaks when they are needed, and varying the work whenever possible, to keep the mind fresh instead of getting bored.
- When enough studying has been done that all the material that can be learned has been learned, and the test taker is prepared for the test, stop studying and do something relaxing such as listening to music, watching a movie, or taking a warm bubble bath.

There are also many other techniques to minimize the uneasiness or apprehension that is experienced along with test anxiety before, during, or even after the examination. In fact, there are a great deal of things that can be done to stop anxiety from interfering with lifestyle and performance. Again, remember that anxiety will not be eliminated entirely, and it shouldn't be. Otherwise that "up" feeling for exams would not exist, and most of us depend on that sensation to perform better than usual. However, this anxiety has to be at a level that is manageable.

Of course, as we have just discussed, being prepared for the exam is half the battle right away. Attending all classes, finding out what knowledge will be expected on the exam, and knowing the exam schedules are easy steps to lowering anxiety. Keeping up with work will remove the need to cram, and efficient study habits will eliminate wasted time. Studying should be done in an ideal location for concentration, so that it is simple to become interested in the material and give it complete attention. A method such as SQ3R (Survey, Question, Read, Recite, Review) is a wonderful key to follow to make sure that the study habits are as effective as possible, especially in the case of learning from a textbook. Flashcards are great techniques for memorization. Learning to take good notes will mean that notes will be full of useful information, so that less sifting will need to be done to seek out what is pertinent for studying. Reviewing notes after class and then again on occasion will keep the information fresh in the mind. From notes that have been taken summary sheets and outlines can be made for simpler reviewing.

A study group can also be a very motivational and helpful place to study, as there will be a sharing of ideas, all of the minds can work together, to make sure that everyone understands, and the studying will be made more interesting because it will be a social occasion.

Basically, though, as long as the test-taker remains organized and self confident, with efficient study habits, less time will need to be spent studying, and higher grades will be achieved.

To become self confident, there are many useful steps. The first of these is "self talk." It has been shown through extensive research, that self-talk for students who suffer from test anxiety, should be well monitored, in order to make sure that it contributes to self confidence as opposed to sinking the student. Frequently the self talk of test-anxious students is negative or self-defeating, thinking that everyone else is smarter and faster, that they always mess up, and that if they don't do well, they'll fail the entire course. It is important to decreasing anxiety that awareness is made of self talk. Try writing any negative self thoughts and then disputing them with a positive statement instead. Begin self-encouragement as though it was a friend speaking. Repeat positive statements to help reprogram the mind to believing in successes instead of failures.

Helpful Techniques

Other extremely helpful techniques include:
- Self-visualization of doing well and reaching goals
- While aiming for an "A" level of understanding, don't try to "overprotect" by setting your expectations lower. This will only convince the mind to stop studying in order to meet the lower expectations.
- Don't make comparisons with the results or habits of other students. These are individual factors, and different things work for different people, causing different results.
- Strive to become an expert in learning what works well, and what can be done in order to improve. Consider collecting this data in a journal.
- Create rewards for after studying instead of doing things before studying that will only turn into avoidance behaviors.
- Make a practice of relaxing - by using methods such as progressive relaxation, self-hypnosis, guided imagery, etc - in order to make relaxation an automatic sensation.
- Work on creating a state of relaxed concentration so that concentrating will take on the focus of the mind, so that none will be wasted on worrying.
- Take good care of the physical self by eating well and getting enough sleep.
- Plan in time for exercise and stick to this plan.

Beyond these techniques, there are other methods to be used before, during and after the test that will help the test-taker perform well in addition to overcoming anxiety.

Before the exam comes the academic preparation. This involves establishing a study schedule and beginning at least one week before the actual date of the test. By doing this, the anxiety of not having enough time to study for the test will be automatically eliminated.

Moreover, this will make the studying a much more effective experience, ensuring that the learning will be an easier process. This relieves much undue pressure on the test-taker.

Summary sheets, note cards, and flash cards with the main concepts and examples of these main concepts should be prepared in advance of the actual studying time. A topic should never be eliminated from this process. By omitting a topic because it isn't expected to be on the test is only setting up the test-taker for anxiety should it actually appear on the exam. Utilize the course syllabus for laying out the topics that should be studied. Carefully go over the notes that were made in class, paying special attention to any of the issues that the professor took special care to emphasize while lecturing in class. In the textbooks, use the chapter review, or if possible, the chapter tests, to begin your review.

It may even be possible to ask the instructor what information will be covered on the exam, or what the format of the exam will be (for example, multiple choice, essay, free form, true-false). Additionally, see if it is possible to find out how many questions will be on the test. If a review sheet or sample test has been offered by the professor, make good use of it, above anything else, for the preparation for the test. Another great resource for getting to know the examination is reviewing tests from previous semesters. Use these tests to review, and aim to achieve a 100% score on each of the possible topics. With a few exceptions, the goal that you set for yourself is the highest one that you will reach.

Take all of the questions that were assigned as homework, and rework them to any other possible course material. The more problems reworked, the more skill and confidence will form as a result. When forming the solution to a problem, write out each of the steps. Don't simply do head work. By doing as many steps on paper as possible, much clarification and therefore confidence will be formed. Do this with as many homework problems as possible, before checking the answers. By checking the answer after each problem, a reinforcement will exist, that will not be on the exam. Study situations should be as exam-like as possible, to prime the test-taker's system for the experience. By waiting to check the answers at the end, a psychological advantage will be formed, to decrease the stress factor.

Another fantastic reason for not cramming is the avoidance of confusion in concepts, especially when it comes to mathematics. 8-10 hours of study will become one hundred percent more effective if it is spread out over a week or at least several days, instead of doing it all in one sitting. Recognize that the human brain requires time in order to assimilate new material, so frequent breaks and a span of study time over several days will be much more beneficial.

Additionally, don't study right up until the point of the exam. Studying should stop a minimum of one hour before the exam begins. This allows the brain to rest and put things in their proper order. This will also provide the time to become as relaxed as possible when going into the examination room. The test-taker will also have time to eat well and eat sensibly. Know that the brain needs food as much as the rest of the body. With enough food and enough sleep, as well as a relaxed attitude, the body and the mind are primed for success.

Avoid any anxious classmates who are talking about the exam. These students only spread anxiety, and are not worth sharing the anxious sentimentalities.

Before the test also involves creating a positive attitude, so mental preparation should also be a point of concentration. There are many keys to creating a positive attitude. Should fears become rushing in, make a visualization of taking the exam, doing well, and seeing an A written on the paper. Write out a list of affirmations that will bring a feeling of confidence, such as "I am doing well in my English class," "I studied well and know my material," "I enjoy this class." Even if the affirmations aren't believed at first, it sends a positive message to the subconscious which will result in an alteration of the overall belief system, which is the system that creates reality.

If a sensation of panic begins, work with the fear and imagine the very worst! Work through the entire scenario of not passing the test, failing the entire course, and dropping out of school, followed by not getting a job, and pushing a shopping cart through the dark alley where you'll live. This will place things into perspective! Then, practice deep breathing and create a visualization of the opposite situation - achieving an "A" on the exam, passing the entire course, receiving the degree at a graduation ceremony.

On the day of the test, there are many things to be done to ensure the best results, as well as the most calm outlook. The following stages are suggested in order to maximize test-taking potential:
- Begin the examination day with a moderate breakfast, and avoid any coffee or beverages with caffeine if the test taker is prone to jitters. Even people who are used to managing caffeine can feel jittery or light-headed when it is taken on a test day.
- Attempt to do something that is relaxing before the examination begins. As last minute cramming clouds the mastering of overall concepts, it is better to use this time to create a calming outlook.
- Be certain to arrive at the test location well in advance, in order to provide time to select a location that is away from doors, windows and other distractions, as well as giving enough time to relax before the test begins.
- Keep away from anxiety generating classmates who will upset the sensation of stability and relaxation that is being attempted before the exam.
- Should the waiting period before the exam begins cause anxiety, create a self-distraction by reading a light magazine or something else that is relaxing and simple.

During the exam itself, read the entire exam from beginning to end, and find out how much time should be allotted to each individual problem. Once writing the exam, should more time be taken for a problem, it should be abandoned, in order to begin another problem. If there is time at the end, the unfinished problem can always be returned to and completed.

Read the instructions very carefully - twice - so that unpleasant surprises won't follow during or after the exam has ended.

When writing the exam, pretend that the situation is actually simply the completion of homework within a library, or at home. This will assist in forming a relaxed atmosphere, and will allow the brain extra focus for the complex thinking function.

Begin the exam with all of the questions with which the most confidence is felt. This will build the confidence level regarding the entire exam and will begin a quality momentum. This will also create encouragement for trying the problems where uncertainty resides.

Going with the "gut instinct" is always the way to go when solving a problem. Second guessing should be avoided at all costs. Have confidence in the ability to do well.

For essay questions, create an outline in advance that will keep the mind organized and make certain that all of the points are remembered. For multiple choice, read every answer, even if the correct one has been spotted - a better one may exist.

Continue at a pace that is reasonable and not rushed, in order to be able to work carefully. Provide enough time to go over the answers at the end, to check for small errors that can be corrected.

Should a feeling of panic begin, breathe deeply, and think of the feeling of the body releasing sand through its pores. Visualize a calm, peaceful place, and include all of the sights, sounds and sensations of this image. Continue the deep breathing, and take a few minutes to continue this with closed eyes. When all is well again, return to the test.

If a "blanking" occurs for a certain question, skip it and move on to the next question. There will be time to return to the other question later. Get everything done that can be done, first, to guarantee all the grades that can be compiled, and to build all of the confidence possible. Then return to the weaker questions to build the marks from there.

Remember, one's own reality can be created, so as long as the belief is there, success will follow. And remember: anxiety can happen later, right now, there's an exam to be written!

After the examination is complete, whether there is a feeling for a good grade or a bad grade, don't dwell on the exam, and be certain to follow through on the reward that was promised...and enjoy it! Don't dwell on any mistakes that have been made, as there is nothing that can be done at this point anyway.

Additionally, don't begin to study for the next test right away. Do something relaxing for a while, and let the mind relax and prepare itself to begin absorbing information again.

From the results of the exam - both the grade and the entire experience, be certain to learn from what has gone on. Perfect studying habits and work some more on confidence in order to make the next examination experience even better than the last one.

Learn to avoid places where openings occurred for laziness, procrastination and day dreaming.

Use the time between this exam and the next one to better learn to relax, even learning to relax on cue, so that any anxiety can be controlled during the next exam. Learn how to relax the body. Slouch in your chair if that helps. Tighten and then relax all of the different muscle groups, one group at a time, beginning with the feet and then working all the way up to the neck and face. This will ultimately relax the muscles more than they were to begin with. Learn how to breathe deeply and comfortably, and focus on this breathing going in and out as a relaxing thought. With every exhale, repeat the word "relax."
As common as test anxiety is, it is very possible to overcome it. Make yourself one of the test-takers who overcome this frustrating hindrance.

Additional Bonus Material

Due to our efforts to try to keep this book to a manageable length, we've created a link that will give you access to all of your additional bonus material.

Please visit http://www.mometrix.com/bonus948/gmg6math to access the information.

R0106865336